CHRISTIAN AND JEW

A SYMPOSIUM
FOR
BETTER UNDERSTANDING

CHRISTIAN AND JEW

A Symposium for Better Understanding

Edited by
ISAAC LANDMAN

New York
HORACE LIVERIGHT
1929

DEDICATED

TO

THE PERMANENT COMMISSION

ON

BETTER UNDERSTANDING

BETWEEN

CHRISTIANS AND JEWS

IN AMERICA

"There is something stronger than an army, and that is an idea whose time has come."—VICTOR HUGO.

CONTENTS

PART II

THE IDEALISTS

PART III
THE PROBERS

ACKNOWLEDGMENT

The editor acknowledges with thanks the permission of the authors, spokesmen and leaders, represented in the following pages, to print their utterances in this anthology of enlightenment. To those who assisted in preparing the work for the press, especially to Mr. Louis Rittenberg, we tender our appreciation.

The illustrations throughout the volume are the work of Ivan Sors, Czecho-Slovakian artist now in this country.

A FOREWORD

There is a lawgiver in the Old Testament who once gave a commandment to his people: "Love thy neighbour as thyself." And there is a Rabbi in the New Testament who reiterates this selfsame precept as one of the two chief commandments. Christians and Jews have been reading these books and repeating this commandment for nearly fifty generations; volumes, expository and exegetical, have been written on the subject by the shelfful; sermons, which if laid end-to-end would reach from here to the seventh heaven, have been preached on this text. And yet, neither Christians nor Jews have obeyed the commandment to love one's neighbour; nor have they ascended to the height of vision sung by their common poet, "Behold, how good and how pleasant it is for brethren to dwell together in unity."

This humiliating circumstance seems to have been constitutional between Christians and Jews, from the very beginning. Ever since Christianity started as a sect in Judaism, there has been no concord, no mutuality between them. For nigh on to

twenty centuries their relationship has been char-
acterised by discord, antagonism, even hatred to the
point of bloodshed. Viewing the history of this relationship, one would suppose that Christianity and
Judaism possessed nothing in common to start with,
and that they are antipodal in purpose and objective.
Only latterly have the intelligent and thinking
among Christians and Jews become aware of this
paradoxical slander in man's religious record, this
baffling scandal in civilisation's chronicle of the
Western world.

Studying the historical background of this anomaly, it becomes obvious that antagonisms which
trace their cause to religion are rooted in prejudg-
ment and misunderstanding. Black obscurity has en-
gulfed the transcendental purposes of both Christianity and Judaism. The starting point is intellectual
confusion: Christianity is confounded with Christians, Judaism with Jews. It is a base misrepresentation to hold Christianity responsible for the evils
wrought by Christians who know not what they do
in Christianity's name. It is a foul perversion to
abuse Judaism for the iniquities done by Jews who
know not what they do in Judaism's name. Men and
women may call themselves Christians or Jews; but
if in the name of these respective religions they have
developed toward each other hatred instead of love,
antagonism instead of sympathy, hostility instead of

kindliness, discord instead of concord, then they misunderstand Christianity and Judaism. They defeat and destroy the sublime idealism which has evolved these religions out of the spiritual and ethical experience of humankind.

Both Judaism and Christianity are inspired by a common ideal and are endeavouring to reach the same goal. What has impeded the progress? What has prevented the realisation of the common hope? What has erected the barriers that stand, seemingly insurmountable, between Christian and Jew? This: a long series of misunderstandings, which must be overcome and cleared away before Christian and Jew can unite hands and join in the enlightened march that will achieve reciprocal respect as the essential basis of ultimate brotherhood—a brotherhood that is not visionary or millennial, but a perfected working code of sane mutuality, with faiths federated rather than creeds militant.

On the part of the Christian there is the crucifixion story in which the Jew is featured as the villain in the Redemption Epic. Then there is the theological concept that the Jew has played his fitful part on the world's stage and should have shuffled off this mortal coil. As a natural consequence of the Jew's persistent will-to-live, though declared dead, he was denied the rights of man among men; he was subjected to restrictions, persecutions and exclusions that drove him in on himself, with fateful consequences that multiplied the misunderstandings.

On the part of the Jew there was first the urge to fight back; then the helpless submission to unhappy circumstance. Forced by introversion to look to his own cultural development, driven to trades and professions that were outlawed by the Church, denied world contacts, the Jew bred traits and inhibitions that forced him to become different—a stranger in countries which he had inhabited for centuries.

To-day, however, every force in human life is being re-examined, re-appraised, re-established on newer foundations. The idealism of the world is again in flux. We do not think as our fathers thought. We do not believe as our fathers believed. Nothing that is deemed vital is fixed. Not a single standard of value is conceived as ultimate.

Is it too Utopian to believe that the boon of the future lies in the destruction of the barriers that separate nation and nation, religion and religion, man and man? To believe in the building of bridges of good-will and better understanding to unite all these in a common brotherhood of enlightenment— the ultimate fulfilment of both Christian and Jew?

America is the one hope in the world-turmoil of hostility and contention where Christian and Jew may come to that fuller understanding which will inaugurate the era of genuine mutuality. Here, where men are free to think and believe without molestation, Christian and Jew might well inquire into the age-old fictions which for centuries have alienated them in bitterness and unfriendliness; might well adduce the facts that will unite them in cordiality and fraternity.

It can not be said that ethnic distinctions have created an unbridgeable chasm between Christian and Jew; for racial differences are spanned by the sense of kinship which unites humanity more and more as the world goes spinning on. Nor can it be said that their religions have wrought this horrible state between Christian and Jew, but misunderstanding their religions: for the true Jew can not be anti-Christian; the true Christian can not be anti-Jewish.

It is obvious that the chief cause of misunderstanding between Christian and Jew is rooted in the fact that Christianity is practically a closed book to Jews, as Judaism is to Christians. Christians still approach Jewish Scriptures, not to judge them for what they are—the record of Israel's spiritual experience—but from the point of view of theology. Jews do not read the New Testament at all. It has been anathema to them from the days when the organised Church introduced Jewish persecutions.

Blame can be ascribed to Jews for their ignorance regarding Christianity. Blame can be ascribed to Christians for their ignorance regarding Judaism. Perhaps this is due to the fact that Christians exalt Christianity above other religions. Perhaps it is due to the fact that Jews exalt Judaism above other religions. And yet both are still steeped in mediaevalism—even barbarism. The adherents of both have much to answer for, since the two religions are founded on the propositions of the unity of God, the love of man, and the golden rule of Hillel and Jesus to live by. But if the time has not yet come for Judaism and Christianity to enter upon the heroic adventure of returning to their pristine teachings, if the time has not come for Jews and Christians to live in accordance with the common ethical and humanitarian doctrines of their faiths, we can at least begin to understand each other. For, ignorance is the cruel sire of fear; fear is the shameful mother of prejudice and hate; and the Christian who hates the Jew is unfaithful to Christianity, just as the Jew who hates the Christian is unfaithful to Judaism.

There is, happily, a trend toward better understanding; there are movements afoot which are constructive and concordant. The chrysalis of a new idea is unfolding: that with no loss to the integrity of a man's conscience or his faith he may seek and stress the groping after God inherent in all religions, rather than challenge the pathways others choose

toward a common spiritual goal. It is indeed en-
heartening that Protestants, Catholics and Jews are
agreed to discuss their disagreements agreeably.

ISAAC LANDMAN.

PART I

THE REALISTS

DISCUSS THE PERPLEXING PRESENT

JAMES HARVEY ROBINSON

(Liberal Thinking as a Virtue)

James Harvey Robinson is probably the outstanding American historian of the day. He has made history as popular at Columbia University and wherever his influence has penetrated as Lytton Strachey has made biography. "The Robinson Cult" continues to intrigue, with a growing absorption in history as development and causation. His best known work, "The Mind in the Making," probes the hidden recesses of the human intellect with a keenness and clarity unmatched. The World War found Dr. Robinson violently indignant over the dismissal from the Columbia Faculty of several liberal professors, his ardent disciples. In 1919, after nearly two decades of distinguished teaching, he resigned· from that well-known school as a protest against what he deemed an injustice to his colleagues. His thought-compelling lectures and writings on mediaeval and modern European history are in great demand, no less than "The Ordeal of Civilisation," which is the latest of his most significant works.

LIBERAL THINKING AS A VIRTUE

BY JAMES HARVEY ROBINSON

WE all seem open minded to ourselves. We prize this distinction, and gladly acknowledge it in others, if they will but patiently listen to an exposition of our views and grant their truth. Those who agree with us are "reasonable"; those who do not are evidently inadequately informed and indifferent or opposed to the light. No one will confess that he is unwilling to learn more than he already knows, or that he would refuse to modify his opinions were good reasons advanced for changing them. We all flatter ourselves that we are willing to be "shown," and that, when "shown," we welcome new truth.

These preliminary observations are not meant to be cynical but scientific. They are statements of substantial psychological and emotional facts which we are constantly neglecting in most discussions of tolerance and intolerance. We get nowhere by denunciation and calling names, because no one is a bigot or fanatic to himself. He is a reasonable, fair-minded creature, knowing enough and brave enough

13

to fight for the right, and defend himself and society at large against pernicious error. No progress will be made in encouraging novel and critical thinking by attacks and defenses. For that is not the way fair-mindedness is produced. Its genesis is hidden, and accordingly the methods for its successful transplantation or dissemination are as yet rather obscure, and demand a far more careful study than they have so far received if we are to make head against what we loosely call intolerance.

The art of propaganda is an old one, long ago carefully developed and officially organised by the Holy Roman Apostolic Church. Its purpose was not, however, the cultivation of open-mindedness but the effectual extension of the faith and doctrines of the Church. During and since the War, propaganda (advertising) has reached its present high degree of perfection but ever with the aim of fortifying belief in the ideas or wares proclaimed rather than encouraging a judicious exercise of one's deliberative faculty. Advertisements—whether of religious beliefs, political candidates, economic tenets, or cigarettes and soap —have in common the absolute assurance that the very best is being offered. And apparently advertising succeeds; at least shrewd people appear to be willing to pay enormous amounts for it. And it succeeds just so far as it adjusts itself to the natural longing in mankind for certitude and comfortable assurances, which may be gained with no painful effort and are handed out complete and lasting.

My own notion of fair-mindedness is: the rare and singular anxiety to find out, so far as we may, how things really are. Traces of this aspiration can, by sufficiently scrupulous analysis, probably be discovered in most human beings. In no one is the per-cent. very high, if we test it by our daily preoccupations. For the most part, these have nothing to do, even in the professional quester, with finding out how any great number of things really are, except as they have to do with making terms with our family and our business. Even those most disposed to seek knowledge and meditate thereon are moreover apt to become attached, through habit or circumstance, to the ever fruitful soil of some tiny field and leave most of their convictions to chance.

Our beliefs are really habits, which are usually acquired insensibly, and not at all as the result of taking thought. This makes them appear to us natural and inevitable when they are called to our attention. So to criticise them seems an impertinence. From earliest childhood we are wonted to authority and taught to look up to it and to neglect it at our peril. Mankind is on the whole a docile, not to say slavish, animal and is pretty readily reduced to routine. (Otherwise what we call a high degree of civilisation could never have come about!) A great part of his prejudices are formed during his early years and never outgrown. It is interesting to observe how many of the opinions hotly defended in later life by the conservatively-minded are those which might readily dominate the mind of a twelve-year-old boy or girl. We use without blushing the expression, "We have always thought," and too often we really have. Loyalty and self-esteem combine to re-enforce habit, so that a conscious desertion of our convictions strikes us as a form of treason for which some vague judge is likely to call us to account—the vague judge being a recollection of the anticipated reproofs of nervous or horrified parents and teachers.

It is curious how neatly the workings of religious education dovetail into this whole situation and give a more enduring quality to childish impressions of truth than they might otherwise have. Jews and Christians have in their sacred Scriptures a fund of God-given information to which the devout are pledged for life. They must "believe the Scriptures," which means in practise such things as they were taught to regard as established, without question or appeal, by the holy word of the Lord. Of course, each generation of believers unconsciously neglects such things in that anthology of ancient Hebrew and early Christian literature as are no longer current. They are entirely unaware of how many things in the Bible they do not believe.

I rather suspect that Mr. Bryan did not believe in witches or accept the demoniacal explanation of disease; he probably tolerated graven images of things on earth and even of those in the heaven above, and he observed the Christian Sunday instead of the seventh day on which God rested from all his labours and so hallowed it. Could Mr. Bryan have explained just how Sunday was substituted for Saturday as the Christian's holy day he would have made a substantial contribution to ecclesiastical history. He may, too, have eaten oysters and even sausages; yet these are forbidden by the Bible and nowhere is the prohibition relaxed. He notoriously neglected Jesus's genial miracle at a wedding—and most Christians have been wont also to repudiate his suggestions about throwing the first stone, and his example in refusing to condemn an unhappy woman brought before him by a scandalised group of virtuous citizens.

A beautiful and inspiring manual of gentleness, forbearance and toleration could be readily extracted from the Old and New Testaments. Reckless judgment of our fellows is specially condemned both by Jesus and Paul. On the other hand the warlike chronicles of the Old Testament, some of the Psalms, and so-called II Peter breathe a ferocious spirit of vengeance on our enemies and those who differ from us in belief.

It is commonly assumed that the ninth commandment forbids lying. The Lord, however, imposed a far lighter restraint upon his worshippers; they had only to refrain from bearing false witness against their *neighbours*. Now, since misbelievers are miscreants both etymologically and in the hearts of the godly, they can hardly hope to be regarded as neighbours and so do not fall under the commandment at all. And this has been the practise of the Christian churches from time immemorial. Christian judges followed the tradition of the pagan judges (of whom Tertullian so bitterly complains) who condemned on the mere name. In the beginning to call one a "Christian" was to imply all sorts of evil and obscene practises, for which no proof was sought. Later, when the Christian forms of orthodoxy prevailed in Eastern and Western Europe, innumerable heretics were persecuted on their names—Arians, Iconoclasts, Donatists, Manichaeans, Waldensians —and were accused with reckless abandon of every type of evil conduct.

Modern heretics include not merely religious dissenters, but moral, economic, political, educational and scientific skeptics. The old habit persists of readily accepting every malicious rumour in regard to their views and aims. They are condemned on the name which happens to be applied to them. An intolerant habit of mind thus works double misfortune. It not only cuts off its possessor from increasing en-

lightenment; it also serves so to deform new suggestions that they appear to the multitude as footless,
perverse or destructive.

Open-mindedness is discredited as "free-thinking."
This has come to seem a reproach, for it is quite
wrongly assumed that a free-thinker is merely rid-
ding himself of the usual restraints on evil conduct,
from which the believer is withheld by duty, the fear
of God's displeasure and the hope of heavenly reward. In our worldly experience we do not find this
theory borne out, and one cannot tell from a person's good or evil conduct whether he is a believer in
revealed religion or not. While Mr. Bryan was ready
to accept the hazardous plea of Mr. Darrow that
the reading of Nietzsche made a youth a murderer in
Chicago, it would be hard to put one's hand on another murderer among the readers of *Jenseits von
Gut und Böse*, while our penitentiaries are full of
those who would confess to a belief in God and the
life to come.

Liberalism—and I have no great love for the word
—may be conceived as the mood of the explorer,
who notes the facts as he goes along. He does not
know beforehand what he is going to find over the
next mountain or across the next river or lake. He
learns as he goes, and adjusts his beliefs to his increasing information.

We have only just begun to explore man's nature

and the world in which he is placed. We have new methods of research which were not available half a century ago. New experiments are being tried on a large scale, and conditions are vastly different from those with which our ancestors had to deal. Dogmas —ancient teachings which are protected in various ways from the fermentive influence of increasing knowledge—are still congenial to a creature such as man. But, while they are sometimes harmless, their chance of being suited to the present needs and best insight of men is so slight that we should have no least hesitation in calling them in question. The open-minded will do this so far as their powers permit. Open-mindedness, like dogma, demands faith and loyalty. It is a lofty ideal and one implying a new type of the mortification of the flesh—a new conception of righteousness and salvation. Whether one strives to fulfill the behests of ancient dogma or to follow those of open-mindedness, he will often stumble and have his moments of contrition and his renewals of faith. But the new gospel places far more onerous restraints on our natural impulses than did the old. It has its promises and its rewards— sometimes its beatific vision, but these glories are as yet for a scattered few. Yet the communion of saints grows daily.

HENRY FAIRFIELD OSBORN

(Science May Link All Mankind)

Henry Fairfield Osborn is concededly the leading naturalist in America. His position in the world of science is attested by the high honour accorded him as President of the American Association for the Advancement of Science. His affiliations with scientific bodies and the list of his treatises on scientific subjects are more numerous than this page could chronicle. Dr. Osborn, however, is best known as the President of the American Museum of Natural History in New York, for the brilliancy with which he writes on subjects in his field, and especially for the mellowness with which he views life and its experiences. He is the author of "Origin and Evolution of Life," "Evolution and Religion in Education," and "Creative Education." He has been honoured by degrees from numerous American and European Universities.

SCIENCE MAY LINK ALL MANKIND

BY HENRY FAIRFIELD OSBORN

IN this present day world the rapidly increasing knowledge of Nature and of man's place in Nature is one of, the strong—if not the strongest—links in a world-wide chain of good-will and better understanding. While I am a firm believer in religion, that is, religion without dogma and without sectarianism, I must admit that religion as it is to-day in the United States is keeping men apart instead of bringing them together. There are, I am told, over three hundred different forms of religious belief in our country to-day and each form is tenacious of its own doctrine and suspicious of, or antagonistic to, every other doctrine. This cannot be true of scientific communities, because, as Huxley once observed, Science abhors a dogma as Nature abhors a vacuum. There may be many religions—there can be only one body of scientific truth.

This is why Science forges a chain which may link all mankind together. I wish I could maintain further that the votaries of Science form a new dispassionate and exalted priesthood, free from the frailties of the priesthood, seated above the strifes and the rivalries of ordinary mankind; such a thought would be ideal but it would not be true, because men of science are subject to all the inequalities of character that beset human nature at large, and it is only the few great luminaries of Science, of discovery, of exploration, of research, that raise mankind to higher levels of truth, to a broader and more sympathetic understanding of the finer qualities and substantial merits which may be found in every branch of the human race. It is of this great moral and spiritual incentive which true Science derives from the contemplation of Nature that I would like to write.

The knowledge of the laws of nature which we call Science has been gained, from the earliest times of the Ionian philosophers of Greece, at great personal sacrifice and with rare forgetfulness of self. If we study the lives of the men who have advanced the science of medicine, from the time of Hippocrates to that of Pasteur; or of those who have advanced the science of mechanics, from the time of Archimedes to that of Edison, or of those who have advanced biology, from the time of Aristotle to that of Darwin, the story is ever the same; genius for observation, personal sacrifice, forgetfulness of self in the cause of research and discovery.

It is the genius of discovery combined with the genius of hard work and of self-denial which, especially during the last century, has completely metamorphosed our knowledge not only of ourselves and of the planet on which we happen to live, but also of the entire universe which surrounds us and of which we are only an extremely small and insignificant part and of which our planet is only an infinitesimal speck. The realisation of this truth, which has replaced the anthropocentric view of the universe, gives us a new perspective of life.

Some years ago a Western politician was privileged to gaze through the new sixty-inch refracting telescope on top of Mt. Wilson in Southern California at a remote nebula invisible to the naked eye; learning of the thousands of thousands of light-years that separated this nebula from ourselves, he remarked to the director of the observatory: "After all, it does not seem to me so very important whether Wilson or Taft or Roosevelt is elected."

It is this entirely new and different sense of proportion, of daily values, of the general significance of life that Science gives which seems to me to be its greatest contribution to concord and good-will between different nations and races of mankind. How petty and insignificant do all human prejudices appear in the face of these marvellous phenomena of Nature! The contests of war and the strifes between

men, political or economic, the struggles for racial
or social supremacy, the passion for the acquisition
of wealth or territory, the conflicting standards and
codes of religion—in brief, the entire drama of human history—appears in our Age of Science to be
mere melodrama or even comedy in contrast with the
new knowledge of the infinitely beneficent forces of
Nature acquired and applied by scientific investi-
gators. One by one the terrors that beset primitive
man, all the evils of plague, pestilence and famine
that raged throughout the mediaeval period, all
physical ills and ailments that have retarded the
progress of mankind, have yielded before the advance of scientific experiment, and doubtless there
are equally powerful conquests to come.

The very essential conditions of the progress of
human civilisation and welfare are wholly free of
the boundaries of nation, race or religion. The spark
of genius may touch now a son of Italy, England,
Russia, then a son of Japan, again an abbé like Men-
del within his monastery walls. The votaries of Science know no prejudices of church, of politics, of
state, but are freemen in the entire realm of Mind,
in the entire world of Nature. Thus through their
common and lofty purpose of scientific discovery,
they may harmonise and bring together in friendly
intercourse and good-will, nations distracted by war
and divorced by economic strife.

In laying out the programme for a new School of Biology at Columbia University nearly forty years ago, I declared to President Low that Biology, like every other branch of science, knows no provincial, national or international boundaries; that it is as wide as the world and as extensive as our planet; that only through the discovery of new facts of such value and importance as to be greeted with acclaim in the laboratories of the world could the foundation of a biological department at Columbia justify itself. In fulfilment of this programme of the year 1890, one may imagine the gratification that comes from the present international standing and repute of this department of Columbia University, as attested by the reception of its researches in every part of the world to-day and by translations of the works of its students into the languages of France, Germany, Austria, the Balkans, Russia and Japan.

With such dissemination of scientific truth goes a very high sense of responsibility in the conveyance of accurate, well-tested, soundly and broadly based scientific knowledge. Whereas in the financial and economic dealings between different nations there can be some reserve, some withholding of information, even some dissimulation, there can be no limitations of any kind in the conveyance of scientific truths.

I would therefore add to the principles of genius and of self-sacrifice and the impulse of discovery a

fourth principle which seems to me the most important of all, namely: *the principle of absolute integrity*. All the men of genius who have finally reached
the front rank in science have been men to whom
scientific integrity and accuracy are paramount to
every other consideration. It is true that certain men
of science on the road to the highest achievement
have been more than once tempted by personal ambition to promote ideas or discoveries of their own
not soundly founded on adequate observation; to
such men is denied sooner or later the attainment of
the crowning point of their career, namely, the universal esteem, love and acclamation of such names as
Galileo, Newton, Darwin, Pasteur and Einstein.

The two moral factors in scientific endeavour—
self-sacrifice and the passion for truth at all costs—
seem to me to be the strongest and most unifying
forces in modern civilisation. They run directly
against the strong tides of human ambition, of selfishness, of prejudice, of ignorance and of intolerance,
and they foster the finer spirit of national and international coöperation and understanding. In this
sense I am a strong internationalist, for in Science I
recognise no political boundaries and am indifferent
to all political divisions. But in the technical modern
sense of the word I have no sympathy with inter-
nationalism as a political force, because I think that
in every division of human society each class depends

for its advance upon a strong *esprit de corps*, upon appreciation and pride in its own best racial qualities and potentialities; strong *esprit de corps* is essential in the home, in the family, in the community, in the state, in the nation, in order to encourage and to stimulate scientific as well as artistic and literary endeavour, and at the same time continue enthusiastic and eager to recognise the achievements of others.

In fact, the true spirit of Science compels us to welcome the achievements of other peoples, races and nations. In my own profession of palæontology, for example, I received the greatest stimulus from the splendid example of the Russian, Waldemar Kovalevsky, who in a too-brief career ending in the year 1875 set the whole world a new example in palæontologic research. So far as the spirit of nationalism and proper national pride is consistent with scientific advance we may cite the case of the noted Spanish neurologist, Ramon Y Cajal, who as a young medical student searching in vain for a single Spanish name in the medical literature of the world vowed that if it were possible the name of at least one Spaniard should appear in the medical lists of the future. To-day the medical students of the world repeatedly find his name in all medical works.

I have dwelt more upon the intellectual and moral side of human achievement in science because this side seems to me that on which emphasis is most needed in our present day and generation. With scientific discovery as one of the great modern aims of human existence, it is commonly believed that the pursuit of science is a career and an end in itself, and that the man of science may disregard the old standards of morals, of conventions, and of religion and may press into new fields of conquest untrammelled by all the moral forces and traditions of the past. No greater mistake than this could be made. A purely mechanical conception of science, devoid of the sense of beauty and without the broad humanitarian principles that regulate and govern human life and conduct, will not either advance civilisation or promote the spiritual and moral welfare of mankind.

Man himself, certainly the highest and most mysterious subject of human inquiry, is infinitely more than a machine, and the future elevation of mankind to a higher plane than it now occupies is quite as much a moral and spiritual and intellectual problem as it is a mechanical one. We must not only conserve and increase the forces of intelligence but we must conserve the intellectual and spiritual ideals through which every great branch of the human race has risen from the ranks and through which the marvelous mechanical discoveries and achievements of science may be turned toward the universal uplifting and betterment of mankind.

JOSEPH COLLINS

(A Passport To Paradise)

Joseph Collins is one of the few Americans one meets to-day to whom the phrase "Man of Letters" may rightly be applied. A physician by training and founder of the Neurological Institute, to the public he is the Doctor who has looked at life, at love, at marriage and at literature. He writes vividly, forcibly, richly. Although he is author of a treatise on "The Diseases of the Brain," he latterly felt the call of belles-lettres. In recent years his pen has achieved a variety of delightful and mellow studies in humanism that have won him widespread attention and recognition as a critical voice in America, at once refreshing and salutary. He hates humbugs and does not shrink from denunciation, although his attitude is generally gentle, constructive and conciliatory.

A PASSPORT TO PARADISE

BY JOSEPH COLLINS

SIN and ignorance are the parents of fear. Fear is universal. Everyone is afraid of something; of pain and disease, of defalcation and defeat, of reality and unreality, of death and of life. One fears for his soul, another for his body, a third for his goods. We admit and realise the potency of fear as enemy of health and happiness, but we make little effort to discover and destroy its source. He who will purge man of fear will stem the tide of impotence and misery as Pasteur stemmed the tide of disease.

Those who devoted themselves to prying into Nature's secrets during the last forty years have been successful beyond the most optimistic imagination. Ignorance is being dispelled so rapidly that we are breathless merely contemplating it. When we shall have made as much progress with man as we have with the world, we shall reflect enlightenment as shimmering water reflects moonlight. There is no encouragement from the past that we shall make any headway with sin. We wallow in it now as we

33

did a year ago, a thousand years ago. It not only fetters our feet, manacles our hands, stupefies our intellect, anesthetises our emotions, but it engenders, develops and matures fear, man's mortal enemy.

Fear of death that may entail eternal torment is one of the commonest fears of youth. Fear of God is said to be the beginning of wisdom, but why one should fear Him who is all compassion, tenderness, forbearance, clemency and mercy is beyond understanding. We do not fear those to whom we owe our being, our worth, our weal; we love, revere, worship them, and we do everything we can to testify our affection and obligation.

Until we have a different conception of God, and a new attitude toward Him, (which is the essence of religion, indeed is religion) fear will continue to corrode, and devour us, and we shall make small headway in overcoming and eradicating fear until we forget or modify the current doctrine of sin. There is small chance that it can be accomplished. Fear prevents us even from contemplating it.

What is sin? No one knows, yet everyone feels that he knows. Some identify it with deviation from the Christian standard of perfection; some restrict it to intentional breaches of moral law.

For me, there is but one sin: cruelty; hurting for the pleasure of giving pain, whether it be with blow or word; but there are many crimes. It is the duty of the State to deal with the latter, that of the individual to combat and destroy the former. Were I a prophet, I should say that *kindliness* to all domestic creation is a passport to paradise.

Sin, for the originator of Christianity, was a "transgression of the law," culpability in act or thought, and the law was to love God, and love man. Any attachment which interfered with a whole-hearted devotion to God was sinful, and especially devotion to goods or Mammon. Inhumanity, hypocrisy, moral barrenness are the sins that cause most complete estrangement; yet these are the sins that are committed every day by practically everyone. What greater proof of our inhumanity could be had than the slums of every large city? Is it not devotion to goods and Mammon for a Church to have assets of upward of fourteen millions of dollars, thirteen of which is in productive real estate? Is it not the most crass hypocrisy to spend millions of dollars in the construction of cathedrals and of temples wherein to worship God when thousands of His images are struggling with poverty and disease in the same city? Is anything more antipodal to ideal humanity than the present distribution of wealth, and was there ever such an example of moral barrenness as the World War?

Priests should tell us specifically how we reject the mercy and love of God. Has the woman who consults me as I write these lines, seeking relief from the suffering and incapacity imposed by shaking palsy, a disease which seems to be a reward of virtue, rejected them? She has borne and reared eight children; she has fed, clothed and educated them from the proceeds of button-hole making; she has conformed to the teaching and ordinances of the Church in which she was born, baptised and confirmed, and now she must submit to immobility and torture for ten or fifteen years unless she is fortunate enough to become hostess to some virulent germ.

To me, the popular conception of God is monstrous. It is alleged He is the perpetual fountain of love, the exhaustless source of mercy, the bottomless sea of compassion; and that justice has its origin and end in Him. But look where I may, I see naught but hatred, cruelty, selfishness, poverty, crime, suffering and disease. How can these be reconciled with a kind, merciful, just God? The customary answer is that it is not given to man to interpret or understand the ways of God, that poverty, hunger, tears and humiliation—the four beatitudes, according to St. Luke—are vouchsafed us to insure salvation. We are asked to believe that the road to true and everlasting happiness is love of poverty and suffering, and then we devote ourselves with all our determination and strength to overcoming them; everyone applauds us when we succeed and displays contempt and scorn when we do not.

When God sends droughts and famines, earthquakes and floods, we are told we should implore Him to do otherwise than He does: it seems to me nothing less than insult. If God is all-just and all-wise, and He sees fit to devastate us with pestilence or destroy us with war, we should accept supinely and resignedly His divine decisions. We do not accept them, however. We utilise the means that science gives us to prevent disease and disaster; we strive to tame and discipline man's predatoriness and to develop in him justice and altruism that wars may be prevented; we endeavour to forecast the heralds of what are called calamities of Nature.

In fact, we avail ourselves of every resource of art and science to thwart what is said to be the will of God, and our conduct gives us no concern; indeed, we boast of our accomplishment and just in proportion as success crowns our efforts in that direction, we maintain that we have advanced the welfare of the world and its peoples. And we are asked to believe that the calamities we are made to suffer are the ransom we pay for the sins of our forebears.

The rector of Trinity Church in New York has stated that we have ceased to be a Christian country and the Christian minority should not seek to enforce its standards on the un-Christian majority. Where is the Christian minority and who constitutes it? Does it make one a Christian to be baptised or even confirmed? A Christian is one who lives or endeavours to live conformably to Christ's mandates. But I have not encountered anyone who does it. Practically, all of the pious Christians I have known were slaves to one or more of the deadly sins: pride, avarice, intemperance, lust, sloth, envy or anger. I have neither seen nor heard anyone endeavouring to purge them save to suggest that they should be humble, generous, temperate, chaste, clean, content and serene.

We are asked to believe that we inherit a tendency to do wrong. Had not our remotest ancestors been so determined to make a hell upon earth for us, we might have escaped original sin. It was a great calamity to mankind that the teachings of Pelagius and his friend Caelestius were not accepted; they denied the racial consequences of Adam's fault, asserted the entire innocence of the newborn, and recognised sinless men before the coming of Christ. The former stoutly contended that each man was responsible and liable to punishment only for his own acts and that divine grace is not necessary for human virtue, that it was within the capacity of every man to become virtuous by his own efforts. It is a calamity too that the teachings of Augustine prevailed against them, and that Calvinism restored these teachings.

Persons in mental distress who seek aid from me

are forever talking about the sins they have committed, dwelling upon their unworthiness, and proclaiming their doom! I do not know that the thoughts they have had and the acts they have done constitute sin, but when I submit a list of them to those who claim expert knowledge of the ways of God, I am assured they are sinful. But I am unconvinced.

Morality and decency will make epochal progress when men and women know how their bodies work; when no one will be ashamed of physiological functions; when no part of the body is considered shameful and in action abominable. But this will never take place until we liberate ourselves of religious hypocrisy and we shall never rid ourselves of that until we formulate a method of worshipping God that is consistent with man and Nature.

We profess a religion which is at variance with science, intelligence and reason, which no one practises, not even its priests, and which probably not one man in a thousand could practise no matter what its reward.

The Saviour of man said, "Woe unto you that are rich!" and our motivation from the day we become sentient is to create and enhance material possessions, and in proportion as we succeed, man and Church applaud.

"Woe unto you that are full!" and every day, anyone who has the means eats and drinks to satiety, and no one points the finger of scorn at him so long as his conduct does not outrage social convention or infract the laws of the state.

"Woe unto you that laugh, for you shall mourn and weep" and we regret every moment when the antecedent of laughter is denied us. We strive for diversion, amusement, happiness; and in proportion as we obtain them we are told that we lay up treasures in hell.

"Woe unto you when men shall bless you," and we exert ourselves strenuously and continuously to gain the esteem and approval of our fellows.

"The road to true and everlasting happiness is love of poverty and suffering." We hate poverty and the sole object of our activity would seem to be to overcome or escape it.

We are told to do that which it is impossible for us to do: to love suffering. When we encounter an individual who gets pleasure from having pain inflicted upon him, we call him a masochist, a monster and a degenerate. In a lifetime of intimacy with suffering I have not met one who loved it.

Scan the road to everlasting happiness as I may, I see no advocates of the divine law or expositors of religion devoted to poverty. I see them living in comfort, luxury even, travelling in private cars or palatial yachts, clothing themselves in rich raiment, fraternising with Mammon, serenading the opulent, caterwauling the materially exalted and struggling for preferment.

The affirmation that the welfare of the soul is enhanced by humiliating, denying and punishing the body has its foundation in fanaticism. A healthy soul is the complement of a healthy body and vice versa. There is nothing so salutary to a healthy mind as a healthy body and the body cannot remain healthy if it is humiliated, hampered and harassed.

We are told not to lay up for ourselves treasures upon earth, but should we not attempt to do so we are looked upon as wastrels and, should we not succeed, we are considered failures. When we succeed, and donate some of it to bishops determined to perpetuate their names by building cathedrals and to missions for the conversion and salvation of heathens, we are assured that we effect a transfer of the treasure from earth to heaven. And though the nucleus of the treasure be from robbing widows, defrauding orphans, crushing competitors, fleecing the unwary, the honourable amend is made by donating part of it to "the Church."

Why profess a religion that cannot be practised? Why not have one that is consonant with man's capacity? Assuming that God made man and that life on earth is a preparation for life in paradise; that the soul is a reality and not a figment of man's fears, selfishness and egotism; that immortality is a wage to be earned not a gift to be accepted, it is incredible that a task, beyond his capacity, should be imposed upon him, a problem beyond his power of solution.

It has been said many times that any one who should attempt to put in operation the whole of the Christian religion would be locked up as a lunatic. But even though it were in our power to imagine a man who would do exactly what its tenets taught without being committed, we should be confronted with the personification of a monster. He would forsake his family, rob them of the fruit of his or their labour, be a constant source of offense to decency, regardless of all civic duties, an outcast and a pariah.

Thus, we are confronted with the paradoxical situation of deriving our most admirable impulses and most elevating inspiration from one of the most cruel and inhuman of teachings: that vicarious sacrifice and monstrous tortures have purged us of sin.

Why not have a religion that harmonises with the knowledge and thought that is vouchsafed us? It is absurd to say that religion is immutable; it has been subject to as many mutations as science itself. We say that love is the great solvent of the world, and yet we frighten our children with monstrous doctrines about heaven and hell. Threats of punishment, possibly, may direct or influence some to righteousness better than any other kind of teaching, but I have never met any who were benefited by it.

Why not have a religion that is practicable? In conformity with science? It is farthest from me to underestimate the value of religious emotion. It is an ennobling and purifying thing and I am sure that religion is essential to mankind. Its code of social hygiene goes far to check disease and keep man sane. Its moral censorship diminishes vices and prevents excesses whose tendency is to destroy the individual or the race. But why not have a religion that is based upon a system of ethics that is plausible and workable, which the best of men can live up to?

I maintain that none of the people of the Western civilisation, of whatever creed, has evolved a satisfactory religion, that is one which satisfies at once that enigmatic possession called the soul, that complex organism, the mind. The religion of to-day, when it conforms to the laws of sanctity, offends those of Nature, and there seems no reconciliation possible between it and science. Were men to believe the truth of the assertion that "God who is the final reason for everything is the scientific explanation of nothing" and make an effort to submit their emotions to their intellect, religion as it is understood to-day would no longer be acceptable in its present form; the same religion, adapted to fit the ever-changing process of civilisation, might be retained, but the spirit and the letter of its tenets would both be changed.

I should like to see a religion of kindliness, commiseration and brotherly love, the very reverse of what is taught to-day. The road of true and everlasting happiness is not love of poverty and suffering, but the love of well being physically, mentally, spiritually, love of one's goods, of one's body and of one's soul. I should like to see the gospel of man's relations to his fellows written in water, not in blood as it has been done so long as history has lasted and which in each succeeding century has become more sanguinary. I should like to see a religion founded in hope, not in fear; one consonant with fact not with myth; in harmony with truth, not with fiction; buttressed in hope not in despair and consistent with the actual revelations of the immediate present, not with the alleged revelations of the remote past.

Our attitude toward God should be one of love, not of fear. Any religion based upon fear is false. Fear destroys religion as it destroys the body and mind of man. It is not too much to say that no God is worth having who must be feared to be kept. The purpose of our quest of God should be to find a resting place for our hearts, a shrine for our love. Our design and determination should be to find and travel the road of self-growth and of expanding life that we may accomplish self-realisation and so attain oneness with God.

CHARLES M. SCHWAB

(BUSINESS: THE CIVILISER)

Charles M. Schwab is the Pennsylvania stage-driver, grocery clerk, and stake-driver, who studied the mathematics of engineering at night and who rose via the Carnegie Steel Company route to the Presidency of the United States Steel Corporation and to the Chairmanship of the Board of the Bethlehem Steel Corporation. It was he who visioned the need of co-ordination in steel-making, and the future of the American iron and steel industry as it might develop if a combination of conflicting interests could displace ruinous competition. For upwards of twenty-five years, Mr. Schwab has been one of the industrial leaders of America. The varied enterprises in which he plays an active part reach out beyond America's boundaries. Mr. Schwab is well-qualified by experience and temperament to discuss Business as a civilising influence on this business-like planet and its efficiency-seeking inhabitants.

BUSINESS: THE CIVILISER

BY CHARLES M. SCHWAB

INTERNATIONAL business has assumed a place of vast importance to world stability and peace since signing of the Armistice, eleven years ago. During the present year definite signs have appeared that the concerted efforts of business men throughout the world to restore economic equilibrium and effect better understanding among men, are at last bearing fruit. One of these signs is the virtual acceptance of the treaty outlawing war. Certainly, some great change has come over the world when it is possible within a relatively short space of time thus to bring diverse forces into harmony on this vital issue.

The fact is that during the past eleven years—the years of reconstruction following the great War—a new kind of force has been at work. It is a constructive and not a destructive force. Instead of conquering by combat, it gains its ends by understanding. This is the force of international business; and while essentially economic, it is governed by a higher conception of economics than has ever existed before.

47

Business men the world over understand to-day that good business depends upon the maintenance of as favourable relations with the neighbours across the sea as with the neighbours of their own communities. Political leaders, too, recognise this force to-day as one which has a very wholesome effect upon the public policies of their governments.

Americans have taken a leading part in this work of reconstructing the world on new economic lines, but the efforts of men like Herbert Hoover, Charles G. Dawes, Owen D. Young and others would be of little effect without coöperation on the other side. The leaders of business and finance of Europe have done yeoman service in their own countries in rebuilding a greater confidence than that which the War itself and the aftermath of War destroyed.

There have been times, of course, when these reconstruction efforts threatened to fail. There were times when Germany felt the influence of the forces of monarchism and Bolshevism, but the republic has stood the test; and the fact remains that Germany has met and is continuing to meet all of her obligations under the Dawes Plan. Relations between France and the United States and between France and her neighbours have reached a higher plane of mutual trust and helpfulness. England funded her war debts and set out upon the gold standard to regain her stability and all but failed on account of labour troubles and business depression, but to-day the British Empire in general and the United Kingdom in particular are headed for prosperity. Italy and Russia have undertaken political experiments radically different from any other established forms of government. They now appear before the world, especially Italy, with bodies politic which have gained considerably the respect of other nations.

Each year finds the civilised nations of the world more cognisant of their *interdependence*, realising that the economic prosperity of their own people is increased by mutual trade with other prosperous nations. The international trade of 23 countries, according to reports of the U. S. Department of Commerce, in 1927 aggregated nearly 24 billions of dollars. The foreign trade of the United States alone is approximately five billions of dollars a year at the present time. We are seeking to extend markets for our exports in order to make our mass production more profitable. But Europe and some other sections of the world are likewise producing and selling on a mass basis. There is inevitable competition and in consequence there is a greater challenge to world business to conduct its commerce with intelligent regard for the interests of others and free from hostile political considerations.

The business men of Europe have found for the most part that large scale production and cut-throat nationalistic competition do not mix. Accordingly, they have agreed upon certain definite principles to be respected by each in the production and marketing of their goods. Thus there have come into being the international cartels which are notable in such industries as steel, aluminum, coal, rayon, dyes and other chemicals. It has been supposed, without foundation, that these new trusts of Europe are a menace to American business.

The cartel movement, in my opinion, is a constructive and favourable move toward the establishment of friendlier relations between nations. It tends to free business rivalry from the fetters of national prejudices and to bring business competition out into the open. The counterpart of the cartel movement in Europe is the trade association movement in the United States which, under the authorisation of the Webb-Pomerene Act, enables industries to compete as coöperating units in foreign markets with groups from other countries.

One very important factor in developing the cooperative spirit among business men has been the international Chamber of Commerce. Some of the major problems, fundamental in maintaining favourable commercial relations between countries, have been studied and attention focused upon them for solution. Some of the most delicate matters, as for instance the removal of trade barriers, have become subject in this way to necessary and harmonious adjustment. The economic section of the League of Nations too should be commended for its undertakings in the study of business problems which make for better world understanding.

No doubt the wholesome effects of international business upon world affairs have been materially aided by the improvements which have been made in international communication. This includes not only means for the transmission of thought but also means for the transportation of people. It is too much, perhaps, to say that present means of communication make wars possible, but it is certainly time to state that they make it difficult to bring wars about.

Take the dissemination of news. Events occurring anywhere are read and discussed in any part of the civilised world the same day, and even in uncivilised parts of the globe, such as the Arctic, we learn of distress through the radio and are able to direct rescue forces in a way that would have been impossible a few years back.

The World War saw the introduction of the airplane as a fighting unit and hastened its transformation from a hazardous instrument of war to an increasingly reliable method of transportation. The impetus given to aviation at that time has been fortunately carried on until to-day aircraft construction has become an important peace industry throughout the world. Aviation has already succeeded in breaking down international barriers.

Two definite results of this greater freedom of communication and transportation are evident today. First, wider transmission of thought is destroying the old provincial outlook of many peoples. Public opinion is becoming better informed and a new regard for fellow-beings everywhere is taking shape. The second result is in the distribution of commodities and the experience of travel. Never before have the ships and the railroads of the world in times of peace carried so much international trade. The tide of travel is definitely on the increase. In a period of fifteen years the mere handful of people who went abroad from this country has increased to hundreds of thousands and most of those who go aboard return with a better and lasting understanding of the people they have visited.

I am regarded as a proverbial optimist. No one can help being optimistic in this world of change, for every year sees some improvement over the last, and in this year the great improvement in international relations is so marked as to cause one, who has these interests at heart, great rejoicing and satisfaction. Much of the credit for this state of affairs belongs to the business men of the world who are working together in a new and effective way to make the world a better place in which to live.

NORMAN ANGELL

(Essentials of the Better Spirit)

Norman Angell is an Englishman who passed his youth in Western America, first ranching and prospecting, and later in newspaper work. He returned to Europe as correspondent of various American newspapers and has since been a frequent contributor to the press on this side of the Atlantic as well as a lecturer in our universities. "The Great Illusion," which was published in 1913, brought him a world-wide audience and his subsequent books deal mostly with phases of the question of world peace. "The Great Illusion" appeared even in Chinese and half-a-dozen idioms of India. One of his most trenchant works is "The Public Mind: Its Disorders and Its Exploitation." His utterances have the detachment of the philosophic spirit fused with accurate knowledge of affairs.

ESSENTIALS OF THE BETTER SPIRIT

BY NORMAN ANGELL

THOSE of us who are impressed by the importance of the task to demolish racial antagonism, should be careful of course not to underestimate its difficulties, nor to misunderstand its nature.

The difficulties are rooted in instincts which in some dim animal past may have been valuable to the race, but which to-day have become so anti-social that the future of civilisation may well depend (I think it does depend) upon our success in "sublimating" them (to adopt the jargon of the time), upon making them subject to a social intelligence. Even in the simpler societies of the past these antagonisms have wrought incalculable havoc. And as the world becomes a smaller place, as the points of contact between groups multiply correspondingly, that is, making every race and creed and colour our neighbour; and as society becomes a more vulnerable machine, as every machine becomes more vulnerable with its growth in parts and complexity, then those antagonisms, if they remain, may well become even more destructive than they were in the past.

If the clashes between economic interests (for herd antagonisms can grow up with fatal facility around other things than race or religion), between classes, rival social ideals, between East and West, White and Coloured, are all to be marked by violent-mindedness of approach, by passion, by prejudices, by these same animal instincts of the herd in f ict, than the anarchies and disorders which gave us the last war and have been worsened by it, will be trifling compared to what an interracial conflict between, say, East and West may provoke.

The gravest difficulty in it all lies in this: evil in this matter can be made to appear as good, can masquerade as good. Evil hates can parade themselves as patriotism, loyalty to racial purity or religious truth, to one's class or ancestry or creed or heaven knows what. It avails little in this circumstance to appeal to right or righteousness, or even good-will, because those caught up by these passions are ready to declare that right and righteousness are on their side; and that good-will goes first to those of a man's own race, own church, own ideas, own social standards. Above all is patriotism—of 100% chemical purity—invoked to fan the hatred of the particular alien of the moment—Jew or Catholic, or German or Negro, or Jap or Wop, or Bolshevist, or Red or

Pacifist or Evolutionist or "atheist." A fanatical conviction that one or another of these groups, or several, are "vermin to be exterminated" may well provoke within our society recurrent strains and stresses beneath which a machine so complicated as society has become may well degenerate into something intolerant, hateful and cruel.

But if the direct appeal to righteousness and even good-will is ineffective, because those who do the damage are doing it in the name of those things, to what may we appeal with some hope of success?

There is one word frequently used in this connection which gives a hint, I think, of the proper distribution of emphasis. That word is "understanding." We must make it clear in our nursing and encouragement of patriotism and loyalty to old ideals, that *understanding*, as apart from emotion, an understanding of the dangers inherent even in good emotions, is a moral obligation; that it is our duty to be right not merely in our hearts but in our heads. Those who are most dangerous in this matter are not evil-minded persons repudiating right, but persons who do not understand what right is. They have not been made to feel the moral turpitude of not having even tried to understand. Often it is true to say that the honester they are the more fanatical they are; the more they are convinced that in their intolerances they are doing God's will—as the inquisitor who tortured believed he was doing God's will.

What has happened of course is that they are obeying the instinct already referred to, and, "rationalising" that instinct, calling upon accepted moral standards for the purpose of that rationalisation. And it may be objected that since these instincts are "natural" they are inevitable. "Human nature is made that way, and we can do nothing about it."

That is not true. It is important to realise why it is not true. The distrust of the alien and the unfamiliar, "the rival herd" is, we may agree, a nature-made thing. But what makes the rival herd, what constitutes alien—whether it is those who belong to a different nation or a different race or a different church, or whether it is those who by their behaviour or ideas threaten what we believe to be good; what makes the category in fact—is not a nature-made thing but man-made, made by ideas and conceptions which are the result of discussion, tradition, suggestion; not biological but intellectual.

In the fourteenth and fifteenth centuries in Europe it mattered little as a rule that a man should be of different race or nation (indeed the latter conception had hardly yet been born). That did not make him part of an alien herd to be hated. But it mattered a great deal that a man should be a heretic. That immediately made him an alien to be hated. The herd instinct gathered around the religious divisions. To-day in Europe it matters little what a man's religious faith is, that he should be a heretic. That does not make him alien. But it matters a great deal if he is of another race and another nation. That immediately makes him an alien.

Now these changes in the direction taken by our feelings have not had a biological but an intellectual cause; due, not to physiological changes, but changes in man-made ideas. The deep "instinctive" loathing of the Huguenot which made the French Catholic of the fifteenth century refuse to sit at a table with him, has disappeared not because human nature has altered, but because certain men wrote certain books and suggested certain new ideas.

If it is true that nature makes the herd instinct but man decides what shall be regarded as the herd, we can perhaps enlist instinct itself on the side of the cause for which we fight, by identifying the herd which is alien to humanity not with this or that creed or race or nation, but with that group of principles or way of social and political behaviour which in fact do threaten mankind. But to arrive at that we must somehow make it a part of our accepted moral code to "stop and think" about, to understand, our dominant social and political emotions.

And this obligation to *understand*—the moral obligation to be intelligent as one American writer has put it—is not one that we think of usually as a moral obligation at all. What we aim at usually in the enforcement of our codes of behaviour is an emotional acquiescence; not understanding.

Take Patriotism. We know from the spectacle of other nations that that deep feeling, however indispensable and splendid, can be vitiated and become a danger. We give great attention to patriotism in our schools—have created a ritual of flag raising, national hymns and much else. We want the child to *feel*. Do we equally realise the necessity of his understanding that emotion in some degree, by becoming aware of the dangers inherent in it? "It is a wicked libel to accuse me of not believing in the Monroe Doctrine," said the ardent Patriot during a time which nearly brought war between this country and Great Britain. "Of course I believe in the Monroe Doctrine. Of course I would go to war for it. I would die on the battle field for it. What I did say was that I did not know what it meant." There was, in terms of patriotic morals, no obligation to "know what it meant." So long as he *felt* about it, he was no worse a patriot for not understanding.

We Anglo-Saxons (it is an Anglo-Saxon who writes these lines) are indeed rather suspicious of intelligence in morals. "Be good, fair maid, and let who will be clever," wrote the typically English Kingsley. The implication is rather that if she is clever, if she understands things, that is, she is not likely to be good; and if good not clever. In any case the plain implication is that it is not necessary for the fair maid to be clever in order to be good. I suggest that she cannot be good unless she is clever, intelligent. (Particularly one might add, in this generation!) A goodness which feels no obligation to stop and think about its prejudices, to apply intelligent analysis to them, is the sort of goodness in which intense religious conviction and weekly lynchings can live side by side.

The obligation which we should stress as a *moral* obligation is the obligation to subject the first thought to examintion by the second. For the prejudices which enlightened minds seek to countervail are in their very nature things of impulse, first thought, instinct. A feeling of that kind which undergoes even a cursory process of examination, introspection about which we "stop and think" even for a little time if the thought is really honest and objective, is a feeling already half destroyed. We see it so clearly as something anti-social that immediately other feelings come into play to counteract it. Once in a theatre a man cried "fire." The audience obeyed their first thought, their instinct, the instinct of self-preservation. They rushed for the doors, produced a jam; ten were trampled to death. There was no fire. It was a false alarm. The ten perished from an ill disciplined obedience to the instinct of self preservation. A few weeks later in another theatre a similar cry was raised. But the manager was present, sprang upon the stage, shouted to the audience to stop and walk in orderly fashion. The intervention was successful. The audience checked their first thought by a second, brought into play in their minds factors—a recollection of the need of discipline—other than first instinct; overcame one instinct by another through the action of intelligence. No one was hurt.

The emotion of patriotism—which is indispensable, which we cannot do without—is in danger of duplicating the unhappy experience of that equally indispensable thing the religious emotion which at one time nearly brought European civilisation to ruin. During the long drawn out wars of religion no man supposed that Catholic and Huguenot would ever be able to live side by side in peace.

Yet that thing has come to pass, at least in large degree. And the great change of attitude in that sphere is proof that these antagonisms, which we talk of as "natural and inevitable," are not inevitable; and that better traditions of toleration and intelligence can overcome whatever there is of "natural" in them. It is this realisation of the moral obligation to think about our prejudices, to be intelligent about them, to rise by our minds above them if you will, which is the outstanding need of the world to-day.

JOHN ERSKINE

(The Young Intellectuals)

John Erskine, that modern Actæon, whose "Helen" and "Galahad" and "Adam and Eve" endeared him to a public that was refreshed by his novel approach toward the classical panorama, is always human and never tedious. Using these old stories as points of departure for his books, he projects the revivified figures in universal terms. Many who have never read his novels hold him highly for his musicianship, and many another to whom he has been mentor in the classroom reveres him as one of the significant voices in the intellectual forum of younger America. His energies are prodigious, and his mental compass, however it may veer, points always unfailingly to truth. His undergraduate lectures once jammed the largest lecture hall at Columbia to capacity—for there is to his every word the full flavour of a passionate heart and a balanced judgment. Now he is at the head of the Juilliard School of Music.

THE YOUNG INTELLECTUALS

BY JOHN ERSKINE

WHAT can be done by the younger generation of the country, particularly by the young students, to break down the race prejudice which still disfigures our national life? It is a queer question to hound us in a democracy such as ours is supposed to be, and it is almost the last problem which ought to arise among men and women who lead the intellectual life. We are supposed to welcome all races to our shores, and to treat them as equal after they get here, and in the world of scholarship it is the scholar's contribution that we are supposed to weigh, not his ancestry.

But human nature is not logical, not even in democracies, not even among scholars, and we might as well admit that race prejudice is strong in our educational institutions from one end of the land to the other. The prejudice, of course, is not always against the same race, but it's essentially the same prejudice—the dislike of seeing people rising in society who are not "of our kind."

Race prejudice in New York is largely prejudice against the Jew. I have had occasion to observe the citizen of supposed Nordic background who sincerely thinks the Jew and all his works a menace to the country. Such men usually say, when they pretend to reason about their feelings, that the Jew will never fit the political and social scheme of things designed for us by the founders of the nation; that the Jew represents always a centrifugal force in civilisation—he likes to break up the established order; and that even if the individual Jew is admirable he always has a number of relatives, and if you accept one you must accept them all.

With these earnest people I think it useless to argue, for they represent a constant emotional tendency in human nature to damn the foreigner and the newcomer. If they were not damning the Jew, they would be using the same arguments against some other race. They had their prototypes among the Romans who disliked the upsetting Greek culture, among the Romans also who felt that our Nordic ancestors were barbarians, and among the ancient Gauls and Britons who had a low opinion of the Romans; and their wisdom is of the same grade as Americans show when they thank God that they are not as other men—not as those Europeans—or as the visiting lecturer from abroad discloses when he mentions the areas of our culture which are inferior to his own. If this sort of attitude is rooted in human nature, we might as well expect it among the young, and in places that hope to entertain the liberal spirit.

I have observed the same mad prejudice in some young citizens of Jewish ancestry. Them, too, I give up as hopeless, so far as the race problem is concerned; they serve to supply at least a shadow of reason for the Nordic insanity. I have talked with young Jews who maintained what they called the ancient faith of their fathers, that they were, and are, and are to be, God's chosen people, and that their mission toward other races is to supplant them or to lead them.

Just what the orthodox Jew thinks to-day about the mission of his people, I don't know, but as a Gentile and as a human being with very cosmopolitan tastes I have not enjoyed the enthusiasm of my young Jewish friends for curing race prejudice by turning it inside out. The Christian who cherishes a race prejudice is false to his supposed religion. Does the Jew have to adopt something like a race prejudice in order to be true to his religion?

These two types of mind—really the same type—I have mentioned merely to say that for them I can suggest no cure. But I add what I am glad to believe is the truth—that such points of view are safely negligible. If we can't cure them we can ignore them. For we must remember that there are large stretches

in American society where the prejudice between
Jew and Gentile has disappeared. From the intellectual world, from schools and colleges, it is dis-
appearing faster than perhaps we realise. It reap-
pears often among graduates of schools and colleges,
after they have made their brief and casual experiment with the mind, and when they are trying to
reform themselves to the social mould from which
they originally came; but among the young students
and among energetic scholars and artists the old un-
kindness is dead or dying. Ten years ago the question
would have excited me more than it does now; I
have been living so much in a world where racial
lines count for nothing that when asked to write this
article I expressed a reluctance to say anything more
about an exhausted theme—I felt that further discussion might reopen sores already healing.

If some Jews and Gentiles are living together in
respect and friendship, what brought them together?
I should say a common interest in something bigger
than their racial pieties. The Jews and Gentiles
whom I have observed in an admirable relation have
a common passion for scholarship, for science, for
art, for education, for the public welfare, or for
some other noble end. The boys who get on well together in college have found a common interest in
some generous field, according to their abilities and
their age; if the prejudice returns on them after they

are graduated, it is probably because they have not found a more mature interest.

Of course, if a Jew or a Gentile says that no common interest could or should be bigger than our racial pieties, he is, from my point of view, hopeless; he will keep up the prejudice instead of helping to end it. He may think that after his racial pieties are properly honoured he can develop an inter-racial good-will, but brotherly love cannot be built out of our second-best enthusiasms.

If I were an American Jew, I should be proud of the intellectual rather than the materialistic achievements of my race. The Jew is supposed to do well in trade; indeed, the legend is that he is surpassed there only by my own people, the Scotch. But in America he is distinguishing himself more and more in the professions, and among any group of college students you can be pretty sure that the Nordics are preparing to go into affairs and the Jews to pursue the things of the mind. If I had a prejudice against the Jew, I should be sorry to see the teaching profession so largely deserted by the Nordics because it doesn't pay well enough. I do regret what seems to me the increasing devotion of the Anglo-Saxon world to exclusively materialistic standards.

But in the intellectual world, as in the economic, I am a free-trader, and I am glad to see those men, of any stock, entering the professions who appreciate the dignity and importance of the mind. The Jew is among the leaders now in the intellectual world; if I were a Jew, hurt by the prejudice of my fellow citizens, I should get some comfort and some humour out of the fact that those same fellow citizens are abdicating to me so fast in the field of education that I must soon be teaching their children what to think and how to think it. But since I am a Gentile, myself indebted to Jewish minds and Jewish hearts for much inspiration and friendship, I prefer to remind the Gentile youth who will listen to me that before long we shall be facing a racial problem much more terrible than this of Christian and Jew. The Western world will soon be at close quarters with the Orient —and in what spirit shall we meet the East? This may have to be answered chiefly by the United States. When it becomes acute, Jew and Gentile will be thrown together, I fancy, in the *common cause*. We may unite our prejudices and pour the whole bitter stream on the unlucky peoples we like to call "backward," or in the face of a real tragedy we may learn to be kind and understanding. It is fascinating to think what a rôle the Jew may play in interpreting the East to the Nordics among us. I have an idea that if we could begin now to study the question together we should find that possibility of service in common which would finish our prejudices once for all.

ELMER DAVIS

(Neither Jew Nor Greek)

Elmer Davis had a rather conventional literary start—for he was born in Indiana. But he has more than lived down the Hoosier tradition. The novel was not Mr. Davis's first love; for, after a brilliant studenthood as a Rhodes scholar, he equipped himself to become a teacher of ancient history, specialising in the classical literatures, including excursions of the spirit in both the Old and New Testaments, as his "Giant Killer" and the essay in the present collection testify. Mr. Davis has achieved a unique position as a publicist. But it is his own experience as a small town lad, as an American and European college student, as a recorder of his observations in the daily press and the magazines, which fitted him to write, in essay or novel form, with an informality and lightness that open up inviting vistas leading towards truth.

NEITHER JEW NOR GREEK

BY ELMER DAVIS

A BRILLIANT Jew, dreaming of a new world-wide spiritual community, said that in it there should be neither Jew nor Greek, bond nor free; but all should be one by virtue of the new spiritual citizenship. The author of that statement was not then very popular with his own people, nor is he now; but, since he has in the long run done more harm to Christians than to Jews, he may be allowed to furnish the text for this article.

Assimilation is never so complete as St. Paul expected and desired; it was not so even in his own churches. Nevertheless, I believe that assimilation is the answer to what may be described, according to the point of view, as the Jewish problem or the Gentile problem. I believe it because so long as we had fairly complete assimilation in America there was no such problem, and in the sections of American society where assimilation is fairly complete to-day there is no problem now.

For instance—

I was born and raised in a small town in Indiana, where among four or five thousand people there were perhaps half a dozen Jewish families, all of the Western European stock. The rest of us thought of them as we thought of the half-dozen Episcopalian families; they were members of a church not numerous enough to have a house of worship in our town, and that was the only way they differed from the rest of us. True, they married among themselves, but so did the Episcopalians; so, in the main, did the far more numerous Catholics and Lutherans and Baptists and Methodists. I never heard of anti-Semitism till I went to college and studied about it as something that had existed in Europe, like feudalism.

The Jews in our town belonged to the lodges and the clubs, and nobody wanted to keep them out any more than they wanted to stay out. There was no religious prejudice on one side or the other; I heard zealous Democrats, in the 1908 campaign, denounce Taft because he was a Unitarian and hence didn't believe in Christ, but I never heard anybody throw that reproach at our Jewish neighbours, perhaps because most of the Christians in town didn't believe in Christ hard enough to hurt themselves. There was no race prejudice; the parents of our Jews had come from Germany, but so had the parents of half the Christians in town.

We did have a race problem, but the objec-

tionable immigrants were what would now be called
100 per cent. Nordics. They were Kentuckians from
the hill districts, several hundred of whom had been
imported to work in one of the factories: a group
visibly different from the rest of us and definitely
lower in culture. The old settlers, the best families
of the town, felt that their intrusion was quite a misfortune for the community.

The old settlers, too, had come from Kentucky,
but about a hundred years earlier. In blood and in
original cultural inheritance the best families and
the new undesirables were alike. The difference was
the difference between Spanish-Portuguese Jews,
who came to America from Holland in the seventeenth century, and Spanish-Portuguese Jews who
came to America from the Levant in the twentieth
century; between Jews who came to America direct
from Germany and German Jews who came to
America after several centuries' sojourn in the Russian pale. The difference was not the fault of the
later immigrants—they had simply been out of luck;
but there was a difference, none the less.

Well, that was twenty years ago. There may be
anti-Semitism in that town now, for it is a strong-
hold of the Klan; but when I knew it, there was no
aggressive religious or racial consciousness on either
side. Differences were between individuals.

And that, I suppose, was the general condition in

the United States up to the last few years. The
Spanish-Portuguese Jews and the overwhelming majority of German and Hungarian Jews were assimilated, in the only sense in which assimilation is
necessary; literally they had become like their Christian neighbours, to the extent that differences were
individual, and not racial, nor religious except as
the various Christian denominations might differ.
The sharpening of racial feeling—on both sides—
has coincided in time at least with the great recent
influx of Jews from Eastern Europe, which not only
immensely increased the Jewish population, but
brought in Jews of another sort.

Some of the best Americans I know are Jews from
Russia or the Levant, but it will hardly be denied
that the mass of Jews from Russia or the Levant,
through no fault of their own, are not much like
Americans of the older stock (Christian or Jewish)
and can be assimilated, made like them, only after
some time. (That is just as true of Christian immigrants from Russia or the Levant, but they are less
numerous.) I am not an ethnologist and have only
an ordinary working knowledge of Jewish history,
but I keep my eyes open as I walk around New York,
and I believe the Jewish race is as much a fiction as
the Nordic race. Unfortunately, aggressive Christians
(or aggressive Aryans or aggressive Nords, if you
prefer that term) believe in the Jewish race, and to

my profound regret most Jews seem to believe in it,
too. It is as if the original Kentucky settlers of our
town and the new immigrants had felt that they had
something in common that set them off from the rest
of the inhabitants who came from Pennsylvania or
Ireland or Bavaria.

As a reporter, I have covered too many factional
quarrels in Jewish organisations in New York to believe in the crude myth of Jewish solidarity as it is
accepted by suspicious or ignorant Gentiles; but still
there is too much, far too much, Jewish solidarity
and, of course, anti-Semitism increases it day by day.
A people attacked in a mass, without discrimination,
naturally draws closer together for defense. To expect it to do otherwise would be to ask for that forbearance which a Jew preached two thousand years
ago, but which neither Jews nor Christians have ever
practised to any extent when they could help it. Yet
it is a fact that just as counter-offensives by Knights
of Columbus against the Klan are apt to incline
neutral Protestants to feel that if they must take
sides they will have to stand with the rest of the
Protestants, so the sort of conscious Semitism which
is created by anti-Semitism only creates more anti-
Semitism.

What is to be done? It seems a platitude to say
that both Jews and Gentiles must stop thinking
about a man as a Jew or Gentile, and regard only

individual characteristics. Yet that is what it comes to. Primarily, just now, the responsibility lies with Gentiles. For example, the national convention of my college fraternity, a few years ago, passed a rule that no chapter should thereafter initiate a Jew—a measure as absurd as it was outrageous, since a single member could keep his chapter from taking in any man, Jewish or Christian, of whom he did not approve, and incidentally a measure which insulted many Jews already prominent and valued members of the fraternity. It was fought hard by the New York and Chicago alumni clubs, but it was carried by the country chapters—mainly from the South; and no doubt many of the men who voted for the rule are willing to damn the Jews for sticking to themselves. Other fraternities have done the same.

There is no defense for that, or for the enthusiasts for restricted immigration who would keep out Jews as Jews. On the other hand, what defense is there for Jews who think that because Jews in Poland or Russia are uncomfortable they should all be let in here—who fail to realise that we have too many half-digested immigrants, Jews and Gentiles, already, and that what we need for some time to come is to let in only a few Jews and Gentiles who look as if they could be digested easily?

A race, long persecuted, has had to stand together; there is somewhat more reason for my Jewish friends

to rush to the defense of any and all Jews than there
would be for me to take the part of any and all Christians, or even any and all Baptists. "Any and all
Jews," is, of course, much too strong a phrase, for
they do not do it; but I think less of this sort of
solidarity would lead to less anti-Semitism. Give the
Gentile who doesn't investigate the impression that
all Jews stand together and he will judge all by those
he doesn't like. This is familiar ground often gone
over, but Christians will be more likely to judge Jews
as individuals, on their merits or demerits, if Jews
judge not only Christians but other Jews that way.

For the most deplorable feature of the revived
Jewish consciousness that has inevitably been stimulated by recent anti-Semitism is this—that too many
thoroughly patriotic and in all ordinary senses
thoroughly assimilated American Jews seem to feel
that they are at once Americans exactly like the rest
of us, and Jews wholly different from the rest of us.
And the rest of us cannot quite understand that. It
seems like eating your cake and having it, too. I
think this sort of racial-religious-cultural consciousness might be a very dangerous thing, but for the
obvious fact that most of the people who feel that
way are essentially Americans, and Jews only incidentally. We have seen other Americans conscientiously cultivating an admiration for the culture of
an Old World people from which they sprang, only

to find in the pinch that the cultivation was artificial and that they were essentially Americans about like the rest of us. I believe that is the case with most American Jews, but not all of them believe it; and I do not think anti-Semitism will die out in this country until the Jewishness of the average Jew means no more to him than that I am of Baptist training and British-German ancestry means to me.

This, it may be objected, is too much assimilation. But assimilation does not mean that a Jew must give up his religion any more than a Norwegian Lutheran or an Italian Catholic. It does not necessarily mean intermarriage, though personally I think it often should (and, in fact, it often does). It does not mean that a Jew must surrender his cultural heritage; all sensible Americanisation experts are now trying to preserve a good share of the cultural heritages of all immigrants—but assimilation comes first.

There is something in the objection that Americans are too much alike already, but what that means is that most of us are too much alike. Some of us— naturally the most recent immigration, some of which is Jewish—are not yet enough like the rest. Mix them all up, keep out newcomers till the mixing has progressed somewhat and the minority will be more assimilated and the majority will show more variety. That is about what we want. Jewish culture is going to be an admirable ingredient in the American mixture, but spread a little of it around among us all—don't confine it to Jews.

What can my generation do about it? Only what I have said already—Jews and Christians must estimate Jews and Christians as individuals, and not by religion or race. Christians must fight every effort to discriminate against Jews (or anybody else); and American Jews should remember that they have on the whole more in common with most Gentile Americans than with Jews of other countries, or, for that matter, with a good many Jews who have lately arrived on these shores.

Is that too much? It was the way Jews and Christians both felt twenty years ago in the small town I have described. And that sort of assimilation—which, it will be observed, is an assimilation of Gentiles as well as of Jews—is actually operative today in the arts and the demi-arts, the newspaper and magazine and show businesses. In that world (with the exception of some few Catholic writers who seem inclined to make Catholicism a meal ticket) a man's religion or his lack of religion is his private business; diversity of origin is negligible beside common present interests. That a man is a Jew is, as a rule, not much more important to him or to anybody else than that he is or was a Presbyterian.

That is the way it works in the arts and allied businesses; that is the way it works in the Socialist

Church where St. Paul's ideal of neither Jew nor
Gentile, neither rich man nor poor man, has been
realised, perhaps, somewhat better than it was in the
early Christian church; that is the way it was working a few years ago in parts of New York City before both sides began to grow self-conscious. There
are thousands of New Yorkers who are not recognis-
ably either Jewish or Gentile in their appearance,
manner or habit of mind; they belong to a local type
which transcends differences of blood and ancestry.
Assimilation of the sort I have described is actually
going on—only, it is not going on fast enough, and
I think we all ought to help it along.

Doubtless to many Jews this seems abhorrent—
it threatens total loss of racial and cultural identity.
Personally, as I have said, I do not believe there is
any such thing as a Jewish race. Culturally the Jews
must give up no more than any other group in
America gives up, and no less. If they must become
less Jewish, the rest of us must equally become less
Gentile or more Jewish, whichever you call it.

And, of course, there is nothing more criminally
absurd than to refuse to let the Jews in and then
abuse them for staying out. It is an old and simple
prescription, but the fact that both Jew and Gentile
need nothing but common sense and a little more
of that charity which may be called Christian or
Jewish with equal propriety.

KIMBALL YOUNG

(The Mind of the Bigot)

Kimball Young has lectured and written on social psychology and personality problems. From 1920 to 1926, he was connected with the Department of Psychology at the University of Oregon, and in the latter year he became Associate Professor of Sociology at the University of Wisconsin, which chair he holds now. Born in 1893, he has already made a marked impress in the field of his work. His recently published "Source Book in Social Psychology" is a genuine contribution to the fundamentals of a subject into which research has only recently been probing. Dr. Young is a member of various scientific societies and writes with vigour and discernment.

THE MIND OF THE BIGOT

BY KIMBALL YOUNG

ABOUT the middle of the seventeenth century the city council of Halle in Würtemberg conferred special privileges on a Jewish physician because of his admirable services and skill. At this "the clergy of the city joined in a protest declaring that 'it were better to die with Christ than be cured by a Jew doctor aided by the devil.'" This little story illustrates very well a bigotry which has by no means disappeared from the world in which men of different religions mingle with each other.

It is perfectly natural for us to like some persons and dislike others. Ordinarily, however, this like or dislike depends upon differences in the habits and attitudes of the other person. Perhaps we dislike the individual because of things he says, or how he says them, or the way he dresses or walks. These negative attitudes are common to all of us from childhood on.

Prejudice means just what it says, "to pre-judge," to pass a judgment in advance of due examination, to form an opinion before one has had experience, to decide a matter without sound reasons. And in prejudice, moreover, this pre-judgment is made for us by older or more influential members of our family, church, or club. In the case of dislikes of ordinary sort, the persons come to build up an individual habit toward the other individual. But in customary ways of doing, the older generation,—parents, brothers and sisters, religious instructors, school teachers and friends—give us the like or dislike ready-made, and we unconsciously accept this like or dislike as our own because it is natural to take for granted as right the things which everyone else in our family, neighbourhood, or church group believes to be so. And the prejudice is applied, curiously enough, not to individuals, but to whole groups of individuals. Thus we call all Italians "dagoes," all Mexicans "greasers," and all Jews "kikes" or "sheenys." And along with these names go other words which describe the kinds of things all these classes or nationalities are supposed to do. Thus "all Jews will cheat a Christian," "all Jews are money-getters," "all Jews are unpatriotic," "all Jewish men try to seduce Christian girls" and so on through a long list of stereotyped statements. Remember that, in this, the personal qualities are left out of the picture.

One of the roots of prejudice toward other peoples lies in the fact that every group of people believes itself superior to all other groups. Americans are taught from the cradle to the grave by parents, school teachers, lecturers, the newspapers, books, the movies and the radio that America is the greatest land in the world, that it is the richest, the finest, the best in every respect.

Likewise, the religious body to which one's family and friends belong teaches that it is the best, that the moral principles taught by its ministers are better than those taught by other ministers, and especially the Protestant sects teach that they are superior to the Catholics, and the Catholics, of course, teach that they are really the only ones who know what the true religion is, the ignorant Protestants having been misled originally by such men as Luther and Calvin, and by their leaders ever since the Reformation. But all Christians, Catholic or Protestant, curiously enough, unite on one point. This is the belief in the superiority of Christianity to all other forms of religion. Similar sets of attitudes are given children about political differences.

Jewish training itself is not free from its own codes of superiority. The idea of the "Chosen People" of Jehovah still persists. So, too, the strong intellectual tradition of the Jew often makes him intolerant of the ignorance shown by his Gentile acquaintance. And many sad cases of persecution by Christians have produced a legend which lies at the basis of the Jew's suspiciousness of the Christian.

Thus, we see that one of the foundations of prejudice lies in the sense of superiority which one group has toward all other like groups: political, religious or social.

Associated with these superiority feelings is the idea that whatever one's own nation, church or social group does is right and what the other group does is wrong. This makes for an easy conscience and for a framework of habits which makes you like members of your nation or church. And in likeness of feeling there is strength.

The matter has still another side. Individuals sometimes recognise that they are not as smart, not as wealthy, not as educated as other members of their own group; but this sense of inferiority and incompetence is overcome very quickly when these same persons think of themselves as parts of the larger whole,—their nation or religious body. Thus, Americans, ignorant and poor or wise and wealthy, take pride in their Americanism. So, too, Christians, good or otherwise in actual conduct, feel themselves lifted above all other creeds in the very fact that they belong to the Christian church. Thus, in imagination these inferior persons find satisfactory substitutes for any ideas they may have that perhaps, after all, they are not quite so important or valuable.

This is a sort of compensation about which the psychologists talk a good deal these days.

The whole matter comes down to the fact that our group, the "we-group," is better than all others. And whenever this superiority is threatened, it is necessary to rally round the banners of words and phrases which describe this superiority and make clear that the *out-group*, or "others-group," is not so good or superior. The idea is nicely portrayed in O'Neill's play, *The Hairy Ape*.

Yet, in daily intercourse of people with one another, one does not see the raw side of this feeling of importance. In order to make clear how this comes into the open it will be necessary to trace briefly the situations which bring prejudices into activity.

In order to do this, I want to introduce you to the word "crisis" in a sociological sense. We talk about business crises, about the crisis in a war and so on. *Crisis* is a word which describes or states that in society a new or unusual situation has arisen and that, if society is to get on in its old and customary way, something must be done about the condition. Thus, in money crises, banks suspend specie payments in order to protect their gold reserves. In a war, a nation calls out its reserve armies to protect its frontiers or to indulge in invasion of the enemy's territory. In regard to anti-Jewish prejudice, as it has grown up in this country, it will be necessary to point out that certain crises have arisen in which the Gentile and the Jew are both involved.

The first of these factors is the coming of large numbers of Jewish immigrants to this country during the past thirty years. So long as only a small number of Jews came to the United States no one paid much attention to them. But as they began to come in ever larger and larger numbers, and especially as they tended to settle down in and around New York and in other large cities, the situation between the Gentile and the Jew changed. A crisis arose. And it tended to take an economic form. So long as the occasional Jew opened up a tailor shop, or a pawn shop, no one cared very much. Rather the newcomer gave a certain business service that could be used, for there was no tendency on the part of the American to compete with him. But as the Jews came on in numbers, they did two things: the better able and thriftier ones began to compete in larger and more substantial businesses with the Americans already in this field. And in the world of labour, the Jew came to absorb almost completely certain skilled and semi-skilled occupations, like the needle-trades. Thus, both the American business man and the American labourer came to look upon the Jew as a pusher and as one who was determined to crowd the native American out of his business or his job.

In a somewhat like fashion, the Jew began to enter our colleges and universities. Now the Italian immigrant or the Slavic immigrant did not attempt to make his way into educational circles. Oh, a few drifted in from the wealthier and older immigrant groups of these people, but not enough to give anyone concern.

But in the case of the Jew, within a generation, the student body of many of our eastern colleges had changed remarkably. This was especially so in the colleges situated in New York City. Even that did not disturb people much until the sanctuaries of education in New England also began to realise what was happening to them. And finally the educational competition came into the open. To-day, we see the growth of anti-Jewish feeling in proportion as the Jews make up a larger and larger proportion of the student body of any particular school. If the Jew wins honours in intellectual pursuits, he at least can be kept from participating in social life. If you can not keep the Jew from winning debating honours, you can exclude him from social clubs and fraternities.

In the field of teaching, the competition is pretty keen. The writer has a very splendid friend from graduate days who was a candidate for appointment in one of the larger Middle Western universities. This man had had years of teaching experience and had already won a name for himself as a scholar

through the publication of important research. When
the head of the department which was seeking a new
professor read his name, he suspected at once that
the man was Jewish. Upon inquiry to men in the
department where this candidate had recently taken
his doctor's degree, the suspicion was confirmed.
The Jew was dropped from consideration at once,
not because the head of the department in the institution was himself prejudiced—he was not—but
because he knew that he could never get the approval of the university administration to the appointment of a Jew on the faculty.

These difficulties for the Jew in business and in
education, of course, do not arise out of the intolerance of the Gentile alone. The fair-minded
Jewish student of the situation realises, I believe,
that the fault rests on both sides. There are Jews
in business and in education who are officious, who
are themselves bigoted, who believe they are superior to the Gentiles. But the problem becomes
socially serious simply because the Gentile puts his
stereotype, his custom-formed picture of the Jew
as a type ahead of his picture of this particular Mr.
A. who is a bit difficult to handle, who is rather un-
duly frank and outspoken and who ridicules, perhaps, the ignorance or lack of business sense of the
Gentile. Plenty of Gentiles do not get ahead in
business or the professions because they are too ag-

gressive, too pushing and too uncoöperative, but we do not have prejudices against business men or professional classes as such but only dislikes for particular persons, the Mr. J. or Mr. S. who is hard to work with.

The matter comes down, then, to the influence of the customary, traditional manner of thinking of the individual Jew not as a person at all, but as typical of a class or group which has certain common characteristics or ways of doing things which we despise.

If we may say, then, that the bigoted and intolerant person in reference to the Jew gets his attitudes and reactions from the customs and traditions which furnish him with the belief in the absolute superiority of his group or religion, we must not forget that this attitude is common to all groups, the world over. We always think our own the best, and the conflict of Jew and Gentile arises because both of these groups have certain values and attitudes which they consider sacred and superior to all other things in this world.

It would be a mistake, it seems to me, to ignore that the Jew has his own sense of superiority toward the Christian. His own religious belief, his worship of the only true God, his being one of the Chosen People, his backward look to Israelite traditions, and his firm belief in final vindication through manifestations of Jehovah, these play a part in the picture too. So, also, the strong intellectual tradition of the Jew has given him a sense of importance that he has, at times, not failed to use in order to impress the Gentile world.

You ask, however, what can we do about all this? There are persons of both groups who are tolerant, open-minded and who are not afraid to face frankly the issue of prejudice and difference. I may venture a guess as to what makes for tolerance. In the first place the tolerant person is emotionally well balanced in reference to people who do not see things as he does. He realises, above all things, that his own group is not perfect, that men have different ideas of right and wrong, good and evil, that some men pray to Buddha, others to Allah, and still others to Jehovah or Jesus, but that in all the prayer, and not its object, is the important thing. The tolerant man does not then take his own group and his own kind too seriously or as free of fault. He sees the good and bad in man irrespective of the labels of race, creed or nationality upon them. He sees the personality first and last; and the group, the class or creed, as only the shadow or background before which the individual stands.

EDWARD A. FILENE

(INTERDEPENDENCE)

Edward A. Filene is a merchant possessed of social vision who pioneered in the promotion of better organisation of production and distribution, and in applying scientific method and efficient organisation to large-scale retailing. To this end he founded and is now president of the Twentieth Century Fund, the purpose of which is to improve industrial, civic and educational conditions. He is the co-organiser of several nation-wide and international bodies, aiming to bring about better understanding between nations through commerce. He served the Government at home and abroad in an unofficial capacity during the World war, and since has been one of the chief American protagonists for international peace. In 1924 he awarded a series of European peace prizes.

INTERDEPENDENCE

BY EDWARD A. FILENE

THE measure of progress is coöperation, not only between individuals within a nation, but between all nations, and between all creeds and races.

There can be no real progress until the antagonisms and fears let loose by the World War have been definitely conquered,—until the citizens of all nations have been given the opportunity of access to a decently adequate supply of the necessities of life, and have been released from the pressure that has prevented their living a creative and contented life. Basic progress to-day, whether material, spiritual or social, depends upon international understanding.

As populations increased within the nations and became interdependent, it became no longer possible to follow the law of tooth and claw, the law of knife and gun. We know that kind of law, that kind of justice, was neither good law nor real justice; that it not only weakened the nation but also made adequate progress impossible. Driven by necessity, with struggle and martyrdom, the individual na-

tions finally embodied the life-saving and life-help-
ing common customs into common law and later
into statute law, and without these it is impossible
to conceive of modern·life and modern progress.

We are now seeing re-enacted on a world-wide
scale between the nations this same struggle for law
instead of war. Modern invention and modern
science have brought the nations of the world together and demand a solidarity of interest. It is
treason to civilisation not to profit from this past
experience. International justice, international law
must come and be cherished and obeyed. It may not
come in our time. We may not be wise enough in
this generation, but it will come—and within this
generation if we will it strongly enough. If we fail
to achieve this, we shall suffer as the men, women
and children suffered in former times before they
willed strongly enough to suppress individual war
and individual violence by common and statute law.

There are still great dangers in the European situation which may lead to another war unless international coöperation, international justice and international law can be substituted for international
suspicion, ill-will and antagonism. If we face the
facts squarely we must admit that the nations of
Europe are not yet at peace. While the Dawes Plan
and the Locarno Agreements eased the tension and
prepared the way for the Kellogg Multilateral

Treaty, there is still mistrust everywhere and a desire in almost every nation to prepare itself defensively against a possible future conflict. Progress towards a basic settlement is not great so long as naval expansion programmes and peace treaties are debated simultaneously.

We are also witnessing an economic war in process, a situation full of peril to Europe, and destructive to the economic well-being and peace of the whole world. Almost every nation in Europe is trying to import as little as possible and to export as much as possible in order to make itself autonomous in case of war, to obtain a sufficient gold reserve to stabilise its currency and balance its budget, overburdened with war debts and increasing military charges. High protective tariffs and political barriers to trade have been built up between nations that are economically interdependent, and the citizens of those countries are being debarred to a dangerous degree from finding work adequate for a decent living. If the strain of these conditions becomes too great for the people to bear the governments will be faced with revolution or extreme violent reaction. Between the nations themselves new wars are in the making because under such circumstances the governments will point out that the fault lies with the other nations who, by barring out imports, have caused these extreme difficulties.

At the same time, as an aftermath of the war, we are witnessing a general recrudescence of racial, class and religious antagonisms. These have been aroused and used by unscrupulous men and demagogues who, threatened with an accounting, have endeavoured to evade the issues of needed reforms by appeals to racial and religious passions. They carry the seeds of new revolutions and new wars.

We in America have committed ourselves to a policy of isolation, but can we remain immune to the dangers of the European situation? We have finally, to be sure, given our adherence to the World Court but it is apparent that we cannot go forward safely unless we take a wiser and more statesmanlike attitude towards European reconstruction, unless we participate directly in the political and social stabilisation of Europe. There can be no permanent progress in a war-ridden or war-fearing world. There can, in the last analysis, be no substitute for war except law—international law; no substitute for international antagonism and fears except international good-will and coöperation.

But international law—effective enough to be a substitute for war—is impossible without an association of nations of which the United States is a member. If the United States, the most powerful of all nations in the present post-war conditions, fails to give its support to international law and sanctions, then the other nations must seek substitutes that will give them assurances of safety. Preparations for defense, treaties of military coöperation and other methods of increasing military power and economic self-sufficiency—the only known substitutes—must come inevitably, have come inevitably, resulting in new international frictions that may lead to new wars. In the meantime, as I have pointed out, international economic wars are destroying the orderly processes of production and distribution, which are basically necessary for a continuing peace. Is not the problem of achieving and preserving the peace of the world, therefore, practically this: "How can the United States be brought to do its share toward the establishment and maintenance of international law and its necessary sanctions?"

The Kellogg Treaty does not, in my opinion, take us far enough into an active participation in world affairs. The simplest, most effective solution of the problem centers, in my judgment, on the United States joining the League of Nations, which is formed on a covenant to prevent war and is now adhered to by fifty-five nations. It was the most practical instrument obtainable for securing peace at the time it was made, and with world conditions as they are it is the most practical instrument obtainable at the present time. This covenant contains the machinery, or the power to create other machinery, to deal with all international disputes or disagreements that lead to war. It also has the machinery to correct its weaknesses. It has already been instrumental in establishing an adequate international court, and fifty-five nations have agreed to submit their differences to this court or to the League of Nations before going to war. If the United States joins the League, no nation or possible group of nations would be powerful enough to defy it by refusing to submit their differences to international law before going to war.

Unfortunately public opinion in the United States is not yet sufficiently crystallised to secure our adherence to the League at the present time. But as the time element is essential in view of the critical conditions in Europe, we must consider such steps as are practical under the circumstances.

The first basically necessary step was taken through the legislation providing for America's adherence to the World Court. The second step, which precedes the third and final step of joining the League, is the passing of legislation by which the United States will agree to join with other nations in applying economic sanctions against any nation which resorts to war without first submitting its case to the jurisdiction of the World Court or to arbitration.

The Kellogg Treaty cannot be considered a decisive step in the development of machinery for the enforcing of peace because its effects must be moral and psychological rather than technical. While it does mean that we have passed a law against war—at least against "wars of aggression"—the Kellogg Treaty has the weakness of any law, however wise and beneficial, that does not provide penalties for its infraction or machinery for its enforcement.

I do not mean to criticise. As a moral force the Kellogg Treaty is immeasurably valuable; it has helped to crystallise opinion that will force the world, eventually, into agreements that are more binding, more effective. As Chancellor Müller of Germany declared at the Ninth Assembly of the League of Nations: "If we are genuinely resolved to renounce war, that resolve cannot fail decisively to influence our conception of armaments."

Under existing world conditions, it seems essential to perfect by agreement machinery for the compulsory settlement of international disputes, forcing nations to go instead of to war to the World Court or to arbitration, and to accept the decisions rendered. The most effective machinery that can be evolved internationally now or in the near future against a nation which repudiates the jurisdiction of the World Court and resorts to acts of aggression, is an economic boycott by all the other nations. It is essential, I believe, that the United States shall agree to join in the economic sanctions, as our failure to do so would make our adherence to the World Court practically worthless and would make the effective application of economic sanctions by the rest of the world impossible. The Geneva Protocol failed on this very issue, for it is evident that so long as an aggressor nation is able to obtain war materials, credits, food and other supplies from the United States the application of economic sanctions cannot be effective. By joining in a policy of economic sanctions with threats of penalties so real as to be deterrent, it should be possible to meet aggressions and assure greater security against war.

This legislation can be obtained, I believe, because the same compelling motives hold good for it that brought us into the World Court. I am convinced that the practical idealism of the American people will not allow us, for the sake of profit, to supply essential war materials and other necessities —without which they cannot make war—to a law-breaking aggressor nation, when the issue is once clearly presented. This idealism has been shown many times in the past in our vote on important questions which involved clear issues of right and wrong as contrasted with material advantages.

It may be objected that economic pressure is cruel to the masses of people against whom it may be applied, but is it not less cruel than the ever-present fear of war, less cruel than the destroying effects of suspicion and hate which this fear breeds, less cruel than the actual suffering and misery that results from war? Economic pressure is force, but a deterrent force, a force to prevent the possibility of that greatest crime against civilisation—war.

It can be rightly pointed out that economic sanctions alone will not prevent war or prevent acts of aggression by a nation that chooses to disregard all threats of these sanctions, and that military sanctions may be necessary. But there is every assurance, I believe, confirmed by outstanding authorities in Europe, that if the United States in addition to joining the World Court agrees not to furnish with the necessities of war any nation that attacks another nation without submitting its case to that Court, then the other nations now associated in the League, will, in case of need and as an act of self-interest, furnish the military sanctions that may be necessary to make the substitution of law for war effective. They will do this because conditions are such in almost all the nations that unless international law with adequate sanctions is established soon it will not be possible for the nations so heavily burdened by the late war to bear up under the huge expenses of military preparedness, unprecedented taxation, and the disruption of production and commerce.

If the United States as a member of the World Court coöperates with the other nations in providing the necessary economic sanctions, then it does not seem practically possible that any nation would unlawfully attack another, as it would then face a complete boycott.

These steps are America's practical contribution to World Peace. The first step has been taken through our adherence to the World Court; the Kellogg Treaty is an encouraging sign that we have developed a "state of mind" for prompting the second step, which provides for economic sanctions legislation, is constitutional, and in accord with our highest traditions. The third and final step, which consists in our joining the League of Nations, must be taken, if we are to assume the complete responsibilities that our position as a great nation demands. Complete international peace is a millennium, possible only to perfect men and through the agency of perfect men, but the important thing is that there shall be a common will to peace, a determination to work with all nations for the ideals of peace. It is only this removal of the fears of new wars and the preparation for new wars that will furnish the sure, fruitful ground on which the next step forward for real and lasting progress can be made.

For my part I believe that we Americans are brave enough and wise enough to help achieve this ideal in our generation.

WILLIAM HARD

(Mediaeval Irony in Modern Guise)

William Hard may be said to have invested American journalism with courage —especially in dealing with the devious workings of diplomacy in Washington and elsewhere. A fearless publicist, he has been alike admired and condemned for his nationally famous exposes. His social mindedness dates back to 1922, when he was head of the Northwestern University Settlement, soon followed by his appointment as Assistant Commissioner of Public Works of Chicago. The late President Roosevelt, in his most strenuous period, found in Hard an able co-worker. A newspaperman greatly in demand, his assignments carried him across the frontiers of many lands. His observations are always free from the conventional veneer and distinguished by accuracy and originality of approach. Many a member of the journalistic fraternity owes Hard the in-inspiration to hew new paths in this formidable estate. His best known works in book form are "The Women of Tomorrow," "The Passing of Theodore Roosevelt," and "Who's Hoover?"

MEDIAEVAL IRONY IN MODERN GUISE

BY WILLIAM HARD

THE feeling against Jews would seem to have two principal roots. One of them goes back many hundreds of years. The other has been developed by modernistic nationalism.

The Jews in mediaeval Europe were the only people to remain within Christendom unconverted and unexpelled. The Huns and the Moors made forays into Christendom and in time were extruded from it. The Saxons were enveloped by Christendom and forcibly converted to it.

The Jews could be converted neither by argument nor by force; and, while in some parts of Christendom they from time to time suffered the penalty of exile, they nevertheless on the whole were able to keep a considerable foothold within the areas dominated by the Catholic Church and were able to keep it without conversion and without amalgamation.

They remained the sole important instance of a religious foreign fragment embedded in Catholic Europe. At that time the question of race was most distinctly subordinate to the question of religion.

Wars between people of the same race did not seem civil wars. Services rendered to a monarch by persons of an alien race did not seem treasons. In the 13th century there temperamentally was a Europe of all Europeans to a degree to which to-day there is no such Europe.

It was a unity resting on a religion. The Jews were a religiously foreign element within it. In the long sequence of tragedies attending the history of the Jews there is none more ironic or more poignant than this: that when the religious prejudice which persecuted the Jew as an unbeliever was abated it was succeeded by a nationalistic movement and a nationalistic prejudice which has feared and persecuted him as a racial alien.

Out of the mediaeval root of anti-Semitism comes the prayer which on every Good Friday is repeated in every Anglican Church in the British Empire and in the United States: a prayer specifically linking together those two apparently supremely lost people, the Jews and the Turks. Out of the modernistic root of anti-Semitism comes the absurd national contemporary credulity which can believe in the existence of a world-wide racial conspiracy of Jews against Gentiles.

No mediaeval credulity could surpass the modernistic credulity which is capable of believing that a whole race can conspire. The mediaeval mind may have been too ready to believe in superhuman possibilities. It at any rate recoiled from some human impossibilities.

Reminiscences from the emotions set up by the coercive religious unity of the Middle Ages still survive among us to plague the members of the Jewish faith. Surely, however, these reminiscences to-day are not so important or so influential as the new poisons set flowing through the veins of society by the excessive nationalism and racialism generated by modern times.

Against these poisons Christianity has not made any struggle notable at all for persistence or for energy. I say it not as a seceder from the Christian Church and not as a critic of its theology but on the contrary as an obedient accepter of its most ancient and established creeds and practises. Christianity on the whole—and the history of the last four centuries, including the history of the late war, completely proves it—has escaped from the unified internationalistic religious bigotry of the Middle Ages only to succumb to the much more infamous little separatist bigotries of nation and nation and race and race.

In our Christian Churches—including those of the historic communion which claims my allegiance—we see along with the chalice which holds the blood spilled once for all mankind the flags which on battle field after battle field have summoned human beings for good causes and for bad causes and for causes unknown to shed the blood of one another. The emblem of universality is accompanied and desecrated by the emblems of separation and mutual hatred.

The necessity of war at times is not one that I am disposed to deny. The necessity of armaments at this time is one that I have taken every opportunity in my power to defend. The elevating of that necessity into an accompaniment of religious faith, and the attempted consecration of it into a feature of the religious life, is no necessity but a continuous capitulation by the Church to the bodily passions of the world.

That capitulation exists outside of the edifices of the Church as well as within them. The feeling against Jews in the modern world cannot be cured by any effort simply to cure the feeling against Jews. The religious obduracy of the Jew has been followed by the racial obduracy of the Jew. Once regarded as a religious stranger, he is now regarded as a racial stranger. He is regarded—in a strong sense—as a foreigner; and the feeling against him can in the end die down only as the feeling against all foreigners—the feeling to which our modern sociologists have given the descriptive word "xenophobia"—is tempered and extinguished.

Christianity cannot encourage its followers to love the Jews and at the same time exhort them to go to the Dardanelles and slaughter the Turks. The clergymen who, because Turks have killed Greeks, would send American soldiers five thousand miles to kill Turks are not going to be successful missionaries of inter-racial good feeling. The emancipation of the Jew from racial and national suspicion and prejudices and frenzy awaits the emancipation of the whole world from them.

I submit that it is one problem. Temperateness toward the Jewish race is unattainable in a world ill-tempered toward all alien races. Good feeling toward the Jewish orientals who generation after generation live a racially unamalgamated life among us is impossible in a Western world which in the name of science can now be almost brought to believe that the efforts of Asiatics to establish self-government for themselves on their own Asiatic soil is a sort of racial sacrilege against the divinely anointed long-headed ruling race called "Nordic."

An infidel could change his belief. How is a poor non-Nordic person going to change his skull? Religious exclusiveness was bad. Cranial exclusiveness is final. We live in an age in which our hatred has been shifted from the infidel who could be cured by baptism and the heretic could be cured by recantation to the foreigner whom nothing can cure.

Accordingly it is not by combating merely anti-Semitism that we can conquer anti-Semitism. It is only by combating all anti-foreignism. It is only by restoring to the races of Europe, both in Europe and in America, a measure at least of the inter-racial solidarity which they possessed a thousand years ago.

To accomplish that restoration, without the religious exclusiveness which then attended it, would seem to be the special duty of the Christian Church, and, if accomplished, its greater possible historic glory. I venture to believe as a fact that the mental and spiritual materials for such a restoration are to be found lying within the Gospels and the creeds. I venture to calculate as a prospect that the death of anti-Semitism requires a certain apostolic primitive resurgence of Christianity.

PART II

THE IDEALISTS
VISION THE HOPEFUL FUTURE

JACOB WASSERMANN

(Folly of Hate and Injustice)

Jacob Wassermann is admittedly one of the most original thinkers of the day. He is chiefly concerned with fictional presentations of themes reflecting the spiritual aspects of life. His searchings cut deep to the roots of human existence and, whether right or wrong, his views command universal attention. Ever since we have learned to know "The World's Illusion," "The Goose Man," "Caspar Hauser," and "My Path as a German and a Jew," we could not but conclude that Herr Wassermann, while somewhat pessimistic, is determined to help make this world a better place to live in. His own sentiments on the subject are as follows: "There are two contending forces in the world—Blut und Geist. Tradition is symbolic of blood (Blut), for its perpetuation has involved the shedding of seas of blood; therefore, it is a destructive element we must all strive to eliminate. It is the spirit (Geist) that produces exalted individuals and makes for love. It is not destructive; it is indestructible—imperishable!"

FOLLY OF HATE AND INJUSTICE

BY JACOB WASSERMANN

SINCE the very beginning of their history, the
Jews have designated themselves as God's
chosen people. All of their legends are impregnated
with this belief and the proclamation thereof. Without seeking the adequacy or inadequacy of the
grounds upon which the belief persists, it must be
evident that a conviction so tenaciously professed
through thou ands of years cannot but impose
extraordinary obligations and responsibilities—impossible of universal fulfilment and conducive to extreme moral tension. This in turn, by virtue of its
inherent provocation, must lead to a calamitous
existence. Moreover, such an axiom, if made the
premise of human existence, is bound to paralyse
moral development, fostering the presumptuous and
making for pharisaism.

It is the tragedy of the Jew that he combines two
distinct emotions within his soul: the sense of superiority and the feeling of being branded. It is in the
consciousness of the constant impact, the friction of

these two currents of perception that he must live
and adjust himself. This, to my mind, is the acutest,
the most difficult and most significant part of the
Jewish problem.

But, viewing it simply and humanly, I contend
that being a Jew renders one not a whit superior,
just as being a Jew cannot constitute a stigma.

It is clear to me that no people can continue being
chosen, nor unceasingly designate itself as such, without upsetting in the eyes of other peoples the normal
order of things. The whole idea is plainly absurd and
immoral.

Alas, it is the recognition of this anomaly that
makes the prospect of every effort toward reconciliation of Christian and Jew so futile, and fills me
with a sense of bitterness.

Every corrupting prejudice begets, as carrion
breeds maggots, a thousand accretions.

It is futile for us Jews to turn the right cheek
when the left has been smitten. It does not in the
least make the Christians (certainly, not those in
Germany) hesitate; it does not affect them, nor dis-
arm them; they will smite the right cheek just the
same.

It is futile to cast words of reason into the din of
frenzy. They say: "What! He dares to grumble?
Shut his mouth!"

It is futile to set good examples. They say: "We

know nothing, we have seen nothing, we have heard nothing."

It is futile to seek privacy. They say: "The scoundrel hides away under the goad of his guilty conscience."

It is futile to walk behind them and to proffer them your hand. They say: "What is he after with his Jewish obtrusiveness?"

It is futile to be loyal to them, whether as comrade-in-arms or as fellow-citizen. They say: "He is Proteus, he knows it all."

It is futile to help strike the chains of slavery from their limbs. They say: "He will surely get his profit out of it."

It is futile to destroy their poison. They will brew more.

It is futile to live and to die for them. They say: "He is nothing but a Jew."

During my desperate youthful days in Munich I had the wonderful experience of visiting the cemetery each morning. There, in the mortuary, I would gaze upon the dead without ever tiring of their immobile countenances. Those waxlike brows, eyes and lips spoke to me. It seemed to me as if all of them were men and women slain by misunderstanding and excessive suffering. In my darkest hours I would come to them with my grievances against the living. To this day I often experience the same feeling. It appears to me as if one can secure redress, justice against the living, only before the dead. For that which the former are doing is utterly unbearable.

But what can they—what can Germany—do about it?

Were I to see a teamster mercilessly maltreating his beast, so that its veins swelled and its nerves were a-quiver, I would answer a possible similar question thus: "First of all snatch the whip from the hand of that barbarian!"

Should I then be told that "the nag is stubborn, the nag is spiteful, the nag merely wants to attract attention, though it is well-fed and the wagon is laden with straw"—I would then still say: "We'll see about that later; first tear the whip from the hand of that tyrant!"

This, I insist, is all that Germany could do. But this would be a great deal. Perhaps even enough.

But what is the Jew to do about it?

This is a much harder question to answer. It is a theme so inexhaustible as to baffle every effort.

Sacrifices are insufficient. Pleadings are misconstrued. Mediation meets aloofness and disdain. Desertion is abhorrent to those of self-respect. Bending the knee brings results only to those susceptible to it—that is, to the weakest individuals. Stiff-necked stubbornness on the part of the Jew presupposes torpidity.

Thus, there remains—what? Self-destruction? A life of twilight, anxiety and unhappiness? Incomprehensible to enlightened and spiritual minds who must choose between enforced loneliness and hopeless strife!

It is best not to think of it.

And yet, there may be a future way out in store for us. Perhaps it is possible to cherish hopes. Perhaps there will come a redemption through Man or Spirit, here or beyond, or upon the bridge between. Perhaps this salvation has already sent its forerunners among us. Perhaps I ought to regard myself as one of these.

At the noon-hour of my fifth decade of life I am within a circle of human figures who seek to reassure me that what has been done was not in vain. I am a German and a Jew, the one as intensely and completely as the other, neither to be severed from the other. I am thoroughly permeated by the elements of both spheres, Oriental and Occidental, instinctively and by preference. It was this that in former days often made me uneasy—very likely because I failed to recognise it. It was, after all, not a product of the will; but of being and of *to be*. It was disquieting also because of the constant call within me to defend the downtrodden, to raise a protecting and a protesting voice.

I am not the sort of man who can render an accounting at will. I can pursue only the course toward which I feel the urge. And as I gradually learned to have faith in the rightness of these urgings, I also felt some measure of tranquillity entering my soul.

In the realm wherein I function everything depends upon whether the minds of people can be entered, affected and uplifted. Not as if I myself were able, God-like, to elevate these lost souls. Not at all. Both he who seeks to open the soul of others and the one thereby affected are alike uplifted by the impulse of love.

For this reason, I am confident that, with the cessation of baseness, the folly and wrath of Hate and Injustice will be rendered impotent—and, indeed, all misdeeds perpetrated will be duly expiated.

Such affirmation is a source of relief to me—and must remind the right-minded of the imperative duty to labour unremittingly for the humanisation of Humanity and to oppose, with all powers of heart and soul, the fateful self-poisoning that threatens mankind. There can be no aim loftier than that of holding up the mirror to our own century,—to reflect therein a true picture of its deeds and import.

(Translated from the German by Louis Rittenberg)

ZONA GALE

(The Robin and the Bluebird)

Zona Gale, perhaps best known for her "Faint Perfume" and "Miss Lulu Bett," has a host of readers. Her novels are veritable etchings stylistically. Although not prolific, she has given us stories and out of them plays, that will endure. There is an exquisite poignancy about most of her works that stamps her an artist in fiction with authentic flair. In her less intense moments she devotes herself to a consideration of human problems outside of fiction —problems that call for no less preoccupation and no less penetration. She has written with incisiveness and feeling on the subject of better understanding because, as a true artist, she feels that the mutuality of human beings in whatever sphere is the pivotal factor in our quest for the bluebird of felicity. Miss Gale evinces, in everything she does, erudition and courage, a creative integrity, that is all too rare today. It is this virtue that will, no doubt, commend her present contribution to the reader. But, of course, one will likewise find in her essay—as one cannot help encountering in her novels—an unstinted fund of truth, pathos, and compassion.

THE ROBIN AND THE BLUEBIRD

BY ZONA GALE

TO approach the subject of relationship between Jews and Gentiles is difficult for those
of us who not often have been able to discern the
differences which certain others stress. Or, when we
have discerned differences, we have valued these.

It is most puzzling. One says admiringly: "The
Americans—so varied in their gifts, able to make
such a variety of contributions to the life on this
continent—so different!" And on the same day, dis-
paragingly:

"The Jewish people—they are different from
Gentiles!"

I remember a day in New York when a friend of
a year or two tried me out. I said that I had lunched
at a certain café that day, and he said: "Were there
many Jews there?" I answered absently: "I don't
know. I didn't notice. I never notice." Chancing to
glance at him, I saw his face shining as he cried:
"Well, I am glad to hear that, for most of the blood
that I have is Jewish blood." I had not known that,
either. But I have friends of years standing whose

church affiliations, whose religious beliefs, whose
parents' nationalities I do not know. And I have
never been able even remotely to discern what differences these could make possibly to me, other than to
interest me, if the differences were sufficiently pronounced. The individual and his reaction to life,
these are all that matter.

Therefore I am singularly ill-equipped to write on
racial prejudice, for I have none and, moreover, I cannot get the point of view of those who have. In races,
in nations, in folk coming from various borders of
the same country, the differences, if noticeable, have
always seemed to me to afford a rich interest and de-
light. But it occurs to me no more to object to others
because they are unlike myself than to object to a
robin because he is not a bluebird.

It is true that there are certain traits in all races
and nationalities which I deplore, as I deplore innumerable traits in myself; but I do not cut off
myself, or the others, because of these. I have seen
acquisitiveness in both Gentile and Jew, I have found
small meanness in both, I have heard loud voices in
public places in both, I have noted in both a certain
arrogance to the other. But also, in both, I have
noted a generosity which has solved impossible situations, in both I have seen quiet and soft speaking
and gentleness and forbearance. Both Jew and Gentile seem to me primarily human.

The Jews and the Christian church have one curious handicap which they share together: If an Elk, or a Mason, or a Royal Neighbour, or a member of the G. A. R. or of the D. A. R., or of any sorority or fraternity, any university or business or professional organisation—if such an one commits an offense, no one ever says, "Isn't that like an Elk, or a Mason or a Daughter of the American Revolution, or a lawyer?" But if a member of the Jewish race or of a Christian church is believed to be guilty of certain kinds of wrong-doing, the immediate reaction is: "Isn't that like a Jew?" or "That's what the Christian church has come to."

You cannot group human beings like that, and indiscriminately blame or characterise them: I feel far nearer to some Europeans, some Asiatics, than ever I can feel to some Americans. Anyone who has been brought much in contact with certain Europeans and certain Asiatics will say the same thing. One then considers only the individual, what he has been able to make of himself, the way in which he has reacted to his surroundings and his fellows, and these first determine his appraisal. After that it is his background and his bringing up, his handicaps and his endurance which should continue the appraisal. And when we have come that far, we begin to know that no appraisal is necessary. All that is necessary is a care that one's own reaction is understanding, sincerely appreciative and ever kindly.

But not tolerant! The word tolerance, like the word gracious, seems to me greatly overestimated. Both connote, or so they do to me, one standing on a safe eminence and tolerating, or being gracious, to those geographically or otherwise *below*. It is the spirit of those Gentiles who say, "Oh, some of my best friends are Jews." This comment makes one wish to complete the unfinished sentence: " . . . and Gentiles and Northerners and Southerners and Canadians and English and French and Germans and Italians and so on, forever."

Who is primarily at fault for the prejudice between Gentile and Jew? Each will say undoubtedly that it is the other. I think that it is unquestionably the fault of both: of the Gentile, who has permitted and fostered a superiority complex—one of the least explicable of maladies, however exercised; of the Jew who has permitted in himself resentment at that Gentile malady; of the Gentile who has made a virtue of his sense of separateness; of the Jew who has made hardly less than a cult of his ancient wrongs.

Of these it is the first and the last with which it is hardest to deal. The superiority complex, whether exercised toward a nation, a race or an individual is a childish affection, beyond the reach of reason. It is the depth of bad manners, masking as anything from self-respect to patriotism—but it is never to be mistaken for the reality of either. It is the opposite of both democracy and aristocracy, for the former countenances no open pretensions to superiority and the latter at least pretends to serve all. Thus the superiority complex has no place in social life and certainly none in religion—and yet it is a disease which actually takes pride in itself. Here the Gentile is assuredly guilty toward the Jew. And if the Gentile examines his own claim to superiority, there are the historical facts which must trouble his assurance. The tremendous figures of the religion which he professes, what does he do about those? I have always wanted to ask a superior Gentile what he does with those great men—Moses, Abraham, Isaac and Jacob, whom Jew and Gentile alike revere. Were Bible Jews so different from other Jews? But then of course I have always wanted to ask a Jew how he can pass over the eternal Sermon on the Mount, preached by a Jew to Jewish people. I cannot understand either of these open failures to do honour to colossal historic figures of any race.

But the fault of the Jew seems to me to lie in his cult—where this exists—of resentment for his wrongs. I know of children of intelligent Jewish families who own to having been taught in their homes to make gestures of contempt in passing a Gentile church. How is it possible that the old wounds and pains should not burn and deepen when

this is true? Many of these children, when they
learn to think for themselves, doubtless discard all
that, but there must be many who are mentally
branded by those early tribal impressions. And since
it is a fact that bitterness breeds true to its own type,
and multiplies, then that which began as a form, as
a mere bitter motion before the door of an alien
house of worship, becomes in time a mental bitterness, and acts its part.

A Gentile teacher in a Jewish school said to me:
"When I first went there, the boys were continually
rehearsing and harping upon indignities which their
people had suffered at the hands of the Gentiles.
They would become excited and angry, and would
in imagination visit revenge on those others. But
after a little time, as we talked together, and as I
invariably said, 'But don't keep it alive. Let it go!'
I would hear them say to one another, with a shrug:
'What does it matter any more? Let it go!' "

If instead of meeting wrong with resentment, the
Jew could learn to have better manners than the
Gentile and meet wrong with indifference, or dignity,
or even courtesy, no American Gentile could with-
stand such an attitude as that.

For any American prides himself on fair play—
how often is that said no matter how often he
fails! And with the generations, he is painstakingly improving his racial manners. When will

he understand that any race prejudice and resentment at its expression are merely bad manners,
raised to an intolerable degree? Socially, and in
family life, in business and even in casual assem-
blages, the people of all the world have far better
manners than ever they have acquired racially. Socially and personally they overlook and make allow-
ances, even though racially they are still largely barbarian. If this is not true, how is it explicable that
Jewish letters, Jewish art, Jewish music are instant-
ly accepted and given their own values and their
own praise? The individual Jewish pianist or
painter or writer is a great man or woman in his own
right, and his race disappears in the eyes of the Gentile. He becomes cosmopolitan, belongs to everyone
so soon as he excels. And in looking back on the history of all art and science, the great Jewish names
emerge and take their places exactly where they belong. Single gifted Jews are lionised the world over.
But these are somehow, in the estimation of Gentiles, extracted from their race, regarded as separate
and not as reflecting the nature of that people—an
unjust attitude not exercised toward any other. And
what a train of great names in art and science this
people can summon from its past . . .

Christians have not always deserved the name of
Christian. One of their most truly Christian attitudes
to-day,—that is, an attitude expressing the spirit of

Christ, would be to express brotherhood toward their brothers, the Jews, who in turn would perhaps then receive them into the same relationship.

The wife of a Governor of a State recently told me that the servants of the executive residence enjoyed, because of their position, a very high caste among the servants of the town. The wife of a New York banker smiled to me over the earnest social distinctions made by the permanent residents in her Summer colony. "It is all relative," she said. So I think that Moses, or Jesus, or a man on Sirius would look at us from the distance now, and smile at the strange schisms, not so much of belief but of blood, among the earth people. Such differences *are* relative. But if one recognises differences, it should be only with interest that there exist such rich varieties of characteristics in our common human race. And there is always the sobering thought that, considered biologically and physiologically, we are all far more alike than we are different. Once, when I made that statement, a woman said to me: "Oh do you *think* so?" and looked amazed.

Someone recently accused me of wanting a new human race. I do. And I believe that I have it. I have it in the thousands of people of all nationalities and all races who now say to one another:

"The purpose of life is to foster the growth of human beings. That is all that concerns us."

CLAUDE G. MONTEFIORE

(The Horns of the Dilemma)

Claude Goldsmid Montefiore celebrated his seventieth birthday in 1928 and was then acclaimed (or condemned, depending upon the point of view) as the leader of Liberal Judaism in the British Dominions. Descended from two families of bankers, Mr. Montefiore troubled the heredity philosophers because he early displayed an avarice for study. Steeped in Hebrew, Greek, and Latin lore and literature, Mr. Montefiore was the first Jew to write a commentary on the Synoptic Gospels. He is also the author of "The Bible for Home Reading," "Liberal Judaism," "The Old Testament and After," and a hundred pamphlets written and broadcast during and after his founding of the Liberal Synagogue in London. Mr. Montefiore has studied Jewish life and religion in America, and is one of the founders of The World Union for Progressive Judaism.

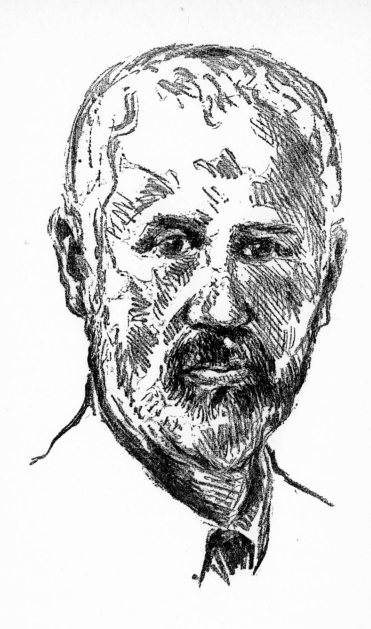

THE HORNS OF THE DILEMMA

BY CLAUDE G. MONTEFIORE

IT is a little difficult for me to write upon this subject. For the need of articles about "good-will"
shows that there exists "ill-will," and this "ill-will"
I have myself never met with or experienced. In my
young days ill-will between Christian and Jew was,
so far as I was concerned, and in my own environment, unknown. In England I thought that it did not
exist, and truly I believe that there was extremely
little of it. I admit that there is more now, and yet
I contend that there is not so *very much* more. But,
personally, I have never experienced it.

If I ask myself: why, in my own environment and
history, was there so much good-will and so little
ill-will, I can only answer that it was, in the first
place, mainly due to the complete separation of national feeling from religious feeling. We were all
alike Englishmen, though our religious dogmas differed. Secondly, it was due to us Jews being no less
keen about *our* religion than our Christian fellow-
citizens were about theirs. We were all religionists.

137

Lastly, it was due to the fact that we mixed freely together, and that each found that the others were very decent fellows, and that there was a very strong family likeness between us!

I believe that these three reasons for the good-will between English Christian and English Jew in those far off days of my childhood and early manhood are still the best specifics for good-will anywhere.

Preachers talk of the brotherhood of man and of "one humanity on earth," as there is One God in "heaven." But it has to be admitted that the presence of a large group of persons, different, shall we say, in colour, in religion, and in ethical and social ideas and ideals, from the great mass of the native population, does constitute a difficulty. It would be ridiculous to maintain that all the race problems of the world are *merely* due to prejudice or to ignorance. But the Jewish problem, as I contend, is much smaller, and is capable of being overcome by ordinary and average sympathy, intelligence and good-will.

The Jews are white people, and they are Europeans. They are at home in Europe, and they, therefore, can be at home in the new Europe of America and Australia. I do not say this in any spirit of superiority or pride. The Indian or the Chinaman or the Japanese may be a better man than the Frenchman or the Dane or the American. But the second three are far more widely separated from any of the first three than they are from each other.

Now the Jew, as I contend, belongs—whatever his race (vague and undefinable concept) may be—to the second three, not to the first. He assimilates quickly. He can soon become good Frenchman, good Dane, good American. He may possess, and for long may keep, certain special virtues and qualities, and perhaps certain special faults and defects, but neither the one nor the other disqualify him from the rights and duties of citizenship, or from the feeling of one-ness with the countries in which he lives. And the special faults and defects tend to become less with the years, while the special virtues and qualities need not *necessarily* do so. For these last depend to a large extent upon his remaining devoted to his religion, while the former do not. Education, intercourse, equality, tend to make him lose the one; they do not necessarily tend—if he keeps his religion—to make him lose the other.

It cannot be expected that all Jews from Eastern Europe—escaping, as many have done, from persecution, disabilities and degradation—could become Americans all at once. It may take two or three generations. But the thing can be done.

It seems absurd to nourish any prejudice against the Jew *as* Jew. The whole point is: Can the Jew be-

come a good American, as he has become a good
Frenchman, a good Englishman? But he has already
become so in America in thousands of cases. Why not,
then, in millions? By good Englishman I mean the
sort of person an average Englishman wishes another
Englishman to be, or the sort of person the average
Englishman considers a good Englishman; not merely that the Jew should feel himself with all the
fibres of his being to *be* an Englishman; that is much,
but it is not enough. He must become, and be, the
sort of person whom the average Englishman regards
as a good Englishman. And such Englishmen have
heaps of Jews become in England, and such Americans have heaps of Americans become in America.
There is no inherent bar. What we ask of Christians
is that measure of good-will, that amount of encouragement, that quantity of what the Germans call
Zuvorkommenheit, to enable us to achieve this desired and desirable end. With that help we can do it:
we can do it quickly and well.

But, then, if that vague word *race* means nothing
serious, if it means nothing which should prevent
Christian accepting Jew, and Jew justifying Christian acceptance, there is, at all events, the difference
of religion. Whereas I have argued that all should
and can go well, if the Jew remains religious, and
religious Jewishly, some would almost appear to
contend that, while he keeps his religion, good fel-

lowship is impossible. Why? Above all, why in
America with its separation of Church and State?

With some people, indeed, on this subject there is
no arguing. Let us hope that they are few. If Christian is forever to hate Jew, because of the part which
some Jews played two thousand years ago in the
death of Jesus of Nazareth, then there is nothing
more to be said. But hardly any educated person
to-day would maintain so ridiculous a point of view.

On the other hand, if there were anything in the
Jewish religion which, from the Christian standpoint,
was unethical or evil, and which therefore vitiated
the Jewish character, or made Jews, as Christians see
things, have low ideals of conduct, then there would
in truth be something to be said for ill-will instead
of good-will. Or, at all events, the only right good-
will would be shown in those various proselytising
efforts which Jews so unanimously deprecate and
deplore. Or even if the differences were great and
marked between the ethical ideals of one and the
other, then, albeit it was not decided or clear on
which side the superiority lay, it might, nevertheless,
be urged that Jews are an undesirable element in a
predominantly Christian country, and that to such an
undesirable element it is impossible to feel good-will.
For one may reasonably desire that within certain
limits there should be a homogeneity of ethical ideals
among all the inhabitants of any particular nation.

But this objection does not apply to the case in hand. Christian ethical ideals are closely akin to, as they are indubitably based upon and developed from, Jewish ethical ideals. Christian Theism is near akin to Jewish Theism. Both can and do address God as "Our Father and King." If there are ethical differences, they are (as I have so frequently urged) not essentially opposed, but complementary. The religious Jew can ethically enrich European civilisation on its own lines. He does not impoverish it. His very Theism, too, to my thinking, though it rejects certain Christian dogmas, contains nothing to which Christians can reasonably demur. On the contrary: it only emphasises (as they think one-sidedly) certain aspects of Deity in which they too believe.

Hence it is that I see no valid reason why Christians should not extend to Jews—the great majority to the small minority, the older inhabitants to the new-comers—the right hand of good fellowship, why they should not feel for them (without straining or effort) friendliness and good-will. But, on their part, Jews must do all they can to *deserve* such good-will. They must all want to be thorough Americans. They must remain religious, and devoted to their religion. And both Jews and Christians (albeit for purely religious reasons they do not intermarry) must meet together in friendly social intercourse as much as possible. Through such intercourse (as well as by other means) they must learn to know and to respect each other. There should be no separation in game or club. That is how we have won and kept good feeling in England; is it impossible, even though, on account of the very large numbers of Jews (comparatively speaking) it is obviously much more difficult, to achieve this ideal in democratic America?

It is apparent, I should imagine, that the fault, as regards the lack of social intercourse, is not on the side of the Jews. Let the Jews, then, be all the more careful about the two other desiderata: (1) They must remain religious and devoted to their religion. Religious indifferentism and religious ignorance must be combatted in every possible way. They are a real danger, just as the religionless Jew is a big bar to good-will,—though I may not develop this conviction of mine in this place to-day. (2) Jews must all *want* to be thorough Americans.

Here some of my readers will smell a rat. "Can he never write on anything," they will say "without dragging in his anti-Zionistic prejudices?" Here, however, they would, I think, be doing me an injustice. I know full well that there are hundreds, if not thousands, of Jews who find no difficulty in combining ardent Zionism with ardent Americanism. They are ardent Zionists, but they are no less ardent American patriots. They are ardent Zionists, but none the less do they feel themselves one with America in aspirations and ideals, bone of her bone and spirit of her spirit.

Such combinations, made clear to themselves and to others, can do no harm. They will not prevent good-will,—the only good-will I am talking about and care for, the *full* good-will which we extend to the fellow-citizen, not the restricted and somewhat chilly good-will which our preachers may ask us to extend to the stranger in our gates or to humanity at large. I am, therefore, not thinking of Zionists—at least not of *such* Zionists—at all. But I admit that I *am* thinking of some Jewish *nationalists*. These I think, *do* prevent the full and true good-will in others, just as they do not seem to possess it, just as, because they are nationalists, they are (as I think) hardly *able* to possess it, themselves. We do not want the good-will of the anti-Semite, who is wont to say that the Zionists (he knows no difference between Zionists and nationalists) are the only honest Jews, because they, forsooth, do not want or pretend to be other than they are—aliens in an alien land, foreigners in Galuth (odious word!).

I am sure I have repeated what I have often said before. But whose fault is that, Mr. Editor? Surely it is not mine, but yours. For *you* asked me to say how I think about these matters, and *I have not changed my mind.*

S. PARKES CADMAN

(UNITY NOT UNIFORMITY)

S. Parkes Cadman is an Englishman by birth and education, an American and a preacher by preference, and the universally famed pulpiteer of the Central Congregational Church in Brooklyn. Dr. Cadman has reached more persons with his spiritual and cultural messages via radio than any other man. As President of the Federal Council of the Churches of Christ in America he rose to international prestige and took advantage of the unusual position to create good-will between Christians and Jews in America. Through sermons and books he has contributed mightily towards the advancement of the ideal of universal peace. He was an outstanding figure at the international occasion which celebrated the Tercentennial of the Sailing of the Mayflower, and at the Stockholm and Lausanne Conferences of the Protestant Churches. He is now President of the American Section for the Continuation Committee of the Stockholm Conference. He is the first preacher in the talking films. Dr. Cadman is a member of the Permanent Commission on Better Understanding.

UNITY NOT UNIFORMITY

BY REV. DR. S. PARKES CADMAN

GROUP strife is the rock on which every civilisation has split. He who cherishes hate is a part of the great conspiracy that draws us into universal struggle about every twenty years and which makes the white man the most dangerous being on all the earth. We have seen other empires and kingdoms, whose names were synonyms for stable government, scattered like leaves in an Autumn gale by this strife.

I do not believe such a fate will visit our country, but I do believe that any nation which usurps just principles, or breaks contracts, or annihilates goodwill, or sets up hate and prejudice and misrepresentation instead of intelligence, education, sympathy, and love as the great motive forces of a definitely ordained society, will disappear from the face of the earth by the judgment of Almighty God. So fell Rome and Greece of ancient renown. So would fall America if she persisted in the way of strife. It is the gulf which would become her grave.

147

As affairs now stand Jews, Catholics and Protestants too often meet to emphasise their differences and minimise their agreements. Destruction lies that way. Our mission should be rather to emphasise our agreements, respect our differences, and labour for the development of a central mind. In the War we had this mind. If it was possible to find it in the business of killing men, surely it is possible to find a common mind in the business of peace. If it was possible for Locarno to declare the reign of peace over Central Europe, then it is more than possible for America to rally around the Fatherhood of God and the brotherhood of man and declare peace and good-will to all in our land.

What shall be the central figure in this common mind of peace? Is it not that sublime gift from the genius of Israel that has made Roman Catholic and Protestant alike her debtor: "The Lord thy God is one"?

Mazzini's last words before he died were, "I believe in God." This is what every Jew, every Roman Catholic, and every Protestant can say. And saying it, all three religions line up together on the right side of the vast abyss.

The consequence of this ideal is the brotherhood of all men. America is the great test case of a nation committed to this principle.

Our fathers of yesterday were of many kinds eventually blended together. To-day the sound of the American city is like that of the "loom weaving the tapestry" of a new mankind. Some of our people are of little faith. They think of America as having failed to blend its polyglot peoples, and as being, not a melting pot, but a "garbage can"; not a nation, but a menagerie. They scoff at their fellows and exalt themselves. There, too, is the way of hate which leads to destruction.

We must trust and believe in the diversified races that make up our land. The Irish, with their mission to nourish the mystic and the romantic; the English, with their contributions for a millennium to law and statesmanship and to the literature and the statecraft of the world; the Scotch, who have built monuments of their thrift and brains throughout the world; the Germans, with Beethoven, Schubert, Lotze, and Kant as their mighty spirits of the past; the Jews, who gave to civilisation the idea of one God, the Father of all, the rock on which is founded every lasting civilisation; the Roman Catholics, who, to quote Principal H. B. Workman, "furnished for seven hundred years the only center of faith and love and light left upon the earth," and who gave to us, through the act of Lord Baltimore, the first American state in which religious freedom was extended to Baptists, Jews and Quakers.

What is the ideal we seek in the American group

mind? Do you say tolerance? Were one to say to his
wife, "Mary, I tolerate you," what would be likely
to happen? Tolerance is a cheap word of political
origin. We do not seek tolerance. We seek brotherhood, understanding, coöperation.

It is possible for Jews and Gentiles to unite. They
do in heaven. I would like to go and see how they do
it. I have often been curious as to the scene when one
finds the other there.

I would not, however, want the various denominations to unite too soon. It would be a case of marrying
in haste and repenting at leisure. Let them first get
acquainted with each other and unite in common
service for great ends.

Then we shall find out, as I did, that some of the
noblest servants of God are among my Hebrew
brethren. I started in thinking God was a Methodist.
But I have had to broaden out.

It is the great business of religion to unite, and
not to divide. To our shame be it confessed that the
church has lagged behind the chambers of commerce,
the community chests, the boards of education, in
encouraging the people of different faiths to work together. But the last and biggest task of unification
cannot be done by the chamber of commerce or the
community chest. It is lasting unification in brotherhood through service, and this must be accomplished
by the churches. Our highest American ideals must

not run merely to richness or bigness. A man or a city which is merely rich or big has gained nothing that endures.

Palestine is a little place, less in population than London or New York, yet from Palestine came Moses, Jeremiah, Isaiah and the Christ. Let our ideal be rather the building of that solidarity of fraternal life in which black, white, yellow and brown, Protestant and Roman Catholic, Jew and Christian are alike parts of the American family.

Unity does not mean uniformity. A lady recently said, to me, "I hope that there will be no differences of opinion in heaven." Heaven itself forbid! Think of saying, "Me too," to all eternity! No. Minorities are the means of growth. Let us encourage differences so long as they contribute to the larger good. Minorities are more often right than majorities. Individuals are far more often right than minorities. Many of them move like blazing stars, counter to the direction of their times. No civilisation is worth while that does not respect variety.

But while we respect variety, let us unite in spirit and service. Let us leave our theological weapons at the door and gather in the temple of brotherhood to do the things about which we agree; take hold as one man of the thorny problems of peace, industry, race relations, in round table discussion, groups and forums, where we can sit, all kinds of us, elbow to elbow. Let us put religion into the schools—not creeds, but religion. No one wants his child's mind to be the dumping ground of twenty creeds; but surely Americans can unite in these practical ways upon the religion of the Fatherland of God and the brother-hood of man.

STEFAN ZWEIG

(The Dove of Peace Astray)

Stefan Zweig is a name to conjure with in the world of European letters. He belongs to the distinguished category which includes Wassermann, Feuchtwanger, Werfel, Schnitzler, et al. He is a dramatist of first rank and a poet of compelling power, his best known original play being "Jeremiah," which is an epic drama of unusual vigour and supreme flights of fancy. His biography of Romain Rolland created an international stir, while his adaptation of Ben Jonson's "Volpone" won for him hosts of American admirers. Almost equally well-known here is his "Conflicts," a collection of penetrating short stories. His preoccupation with the vital problems of humanity is amply attested in the essay here reproduced. Elsewhere he has expressed himself pithily on that which is closest to his heart: "Peace is better than honour; suffering preferable to death." Much of the inspiration in Zweig's works has been derived from avid reading of the Bible.

THE DOVE OF PEACE ASTRAY

BY STEFAN ZWEIG

IN the Book of Genesis is told the tale of the first dove, as also of the second, sent forth from the Ark by our forefather Noah, "to see if the waters were abated from off the face of the ground." That was immediately as the floodgates of Heaven closed and the fountains of the deep were drained. But no one has ever revealed the fate of the third dove.

It is written that Noah's battered craft was finally stranded upon the summit of Mount Ararat and within its lap reposed the survival of the deluge by humankind and beasts. And as our forebear at the mast of the Ark glimpsed nothing but surging billows, endless stretches of water, he despatched a dove, the first dove, to ascertain whether land could be sighted under the cloud-lined heavens.

The first dove, so it is recorded, soared forth on outspread wings. She flew to the East, then to the West, but encountered water everywhere, no place to rest her weary feet; gradually her wings grew numb. Thereupon she returned to the one stable

shelter in all the world, back to the Ark, fluttered
about the vessel until Noah stretched forth his hand
and took the dove onto himself within the Ark.

Thus he waited seven days; seven days during
which it rained no longer and the waters receded.
Then he took another dove, the second, and sent
her on a journey of investigation. The dove flew
forth in the morning and, upon returning at even-
tide, bore in her beak the first token of a liberated
earth, an olive leaf. Hence Noah concluded that the
tree-tops had already risen above the waters and that
the proof of it promised permanence.

After the lapse of seven additional days, he despatched another dove, the third, to ascertain conditions, and this one flew out into the world. She had
left in the morning, but did not return at sunset.
Thus our ancestor knew that the earth was now free
and the waters out of sight. But never again did
Noah hear from this dove, the third. Nor has mankind heard the legend revealed to this very day.

But following is the story of the journey and fate
of the third dove. In the morning she flew out of the
dark chamber of the vessel, in the darkness of which
herded animals bellowed in sullen impatience. There
was a crowding of hoofs and claws, a panicky din
of roaring, whistling, hissing and baying. And so the
dove had flown out of oppressive confinement into
endless space, from darkness into light. But as she

soared into the radiant, rain-scented air, she was suddenly overwhelmed by a sense of freedom and by the grace of the Infinite. Down in the depths below were shimmering waters, and dewy moss lent the forests a glint of green. From the meadows there arose early vapours and the fragrance of plants permeated the fields. The glitter of a metallic sky was reflected from above; upon the mountain-tops played the rays of a rising sun in an endless variety of crimson. The seas were painted a bloody hue, while the blossoming earth was steaming like warm blood. It was sublime, this spectacle of reawakening. Blissfully the dove soared on outspread wings over a purple world, over land and sea, and flew as in a dream that gradually made her flight a dream itself. Like God Himself, she saw at last the liberated earth, and its fascination was overpowering.

The dove had long forgotten Noah, the greybeard of the Ark, and her mission; she had long forgotten to think of returning. For it was this, the whole world, that she felt to be her Fatherland, and the sky her most exclusive dwelling.

And so flew the third dove, faithless messenger of our forebear. On and on she soared over an empty world, swept on by the impetus of her good fortune, by the winds of her blissful restlessness. Farther and farther she flew until her wings grew numb and her feathers like lead. The earth began to draw her down

to itself with irresistible force. Deeper and deeper
sank her tired wings, so that they touched the moist
peaks of the trees, and by sundown of the following
day the dove permitted herself to descend somewhere deep in the woods, which were as yet nameless
—like all else at the time. She hid in the dense
foliage and sought respite from her exultant flight.
She covered herself and was lulled to sleep by the
wind. The foliage was cool by day, and warm was
the dove's forest retreat at night. Presently she for-
got the wind-swept skies and the lure of distance.
The verdant vault enfolded her and time grew end-
lessly over her.

It was a forest of our immediate world that the
lost dove had chosen as her haven, but as yet no
human beings dwelt within it; and so this solitude
gradually rendered her dream-like. She nestled in
the darkness of green nights and the years sped by,
so that Death itself overlooked her. For all animals
of the species known to the world prior to the Deluge
could not die, and they possessed no hunter who
could invisibly remain hidden in the fathomless
earth-clothes, as did this dove in the forest depths.

To be sure, now and then thoughts of this dove
would enter the minds of human beings of the present. The explosion of a firearm might reverberate
a hundredfold from the green walls, wood-choppers
might strike against the trunks, menacing the spell

of the night; the laughter of lovers, furtively strolling through unbeaten paths, might re-echo familiarly through foliage. And the song of children, bent on bear hunting, dimly sounding in the distance. Now and then, the vanished dove, enmeshed in a world of foliage and dream, would hear these sounds of the outer world, but without perturbation.

Then one day, in our own time, the whole forest began to rumble and thunder, as the earth was rent in twain. Black metallic objects hurtled whizzing through the air and wherever they dropped, the earth leapt shattered in the air, and the trees crashed to earth like corn stalks. People in coloured uniforms hurled death at each other and dreadful machines belched fire and blight. Shafts of lightning, accompanied by thunder, issued from the earth toward the clouds; it was as though the earth were eager to leap at the sky or as though the sky were about to smother the earth. The dove awoke from her dream. Death and annihilation were upon her; as the waters of yore, so now it was fire that threatened to inundate the universe. Hastily she spread her wings and soared up high to find for herself a homeland other than the devastated forest, a land of peace.

The dove rose high and flew over our world, in quest of peace; but wherever she flew she encountered the same thunder and lightning of human beings—war everywhere. It was a sea of fire and

blood that flooded the earth, as once before; again a
Deluge had come, and the dove precipitately winged
through our regions, seeking a State of rest and then
to fly back to our forebear in order to deliver to him
the olive leaf of the Promised Land. But nowhere,
in our day, was such a place to be found; higher and
higher rose the tide of destruction about mankind;
farther and farther spread the conflagration through
our world. And still the dove could find no place to
rest, nor mankind its coveted peace.

No one in our day has seen her, this mystic dove
astray; yet she still flutters over our heads, anxiously
and with flagging wings. Occasionally, during nights
only, when one is startled from his dreams, a droning
is heard in the air, the sound of hasty pursuit in the
dark, disturbed passage and frantic flight.

Upon those wings soar all our thoughts, in their
anxiety are centered all our yearnings. She who
tremblingly hovers between earth and sky, the dove
gone astray, as the faithless messenger of yore, com-
municates our own destiny to the forefather of mankind. Once again, as thousands of years ago, an
anxious world waits for someone to stretch forth a
helping hand in token of the hope that the wandering dove may now return from her eternal quest.

(Translated from the German by Louis Rittenberg)

STEPHEN S. WISE

(Calculated Unfriendliness)

*Stephen S. Wise has been appraised as
"the priest in politics, the prophet in the
marketplace, the religionist in public life."
For more than thirty-five years he has been
a picturesque fighter, seemingly seeking out
unpopular causes to make them his own.
He championed woman suffrage, Zionism,
and prohibition in New York; and he
wages intrepid and unceasing warfare
against iniquity, injustice and oppression.
Dr. Wise was brought to America in infancy. His education led through New
York schools and colleges to a Ph.D. degree from Columbia. For seven years he
served as Rabbi in New York; for six years
in Portland, Oregon; and in 1907 he
founded the Free Synagogue in New York.
He organised the Oregon State Conference
of Charities and Corrections, the Zionist
Organisation of America, and the Jewish
Institute of Religion, of which he is the
first president. Notwithstanding his many
exacting responsibilities, he has found time
to publish many of his sermons and ad-
dresses, and to write several books.*

CALCULATED UNFRIENDLINESS

BY DR. STEPHEN S. WISE

IN a moment of distress, touching a serious problem in the nation which involves the adulteration
of our religious life and the lowering of our moral
standards, I turned to one of the truly prophetic
teachers of religion in our land, and his answer was,
"You cannot fight a fog."

One must wait until the sunshine dissipates the
fog, until the sunlight of higher intelligence and
finer sympathy dispels the mist of prejudice and ill-
will. It should not be forgotten that there are some
things so illusive and indefinable, however evil, that
they cannot be fought. The policy of calculated unfriendliness toward the Jew, however, must be
fought, but the weapons to be wielded by Jews or
Christians are not carnal or outward, but inward and
spiritual.

Prejudice and ill-will toward the Jew represents
a world attitude which for centuries has stimulated
the Jew's spirit of forbearance toward them that
wronged us. What Heine said in daringly irreverent
jest of God,—that He would pardon, for that is His

business,—might more fittingly have been said of
the Jew who has come to command the divinest of
human arts, the art of forgiveness, bettering the lesson which Christendom unhappily for itself commended to the soul of the Jew, not by compelling
observance but oft and again by repelling breach.

Greatest of the gains which accrued to the Jew
from persecution and discrimination was the necessity under which the Jew found himself of making
a decisive choice, the choice between the feebleness
of self-obliteration and the strength of self-insis-
tence. The frail among our fathers committed suicide
in one way or another under the intolerable pressure
of a pitiless world. The unyielding and the unstoop-
ing among our forebears lifted themselves up to a
resolution which meant much to the spiritual fortunes of the human race as well as to our own destinies as a people—the ennobling resolution to live
and not to die, the resolution more nobly to live,
despite the challenge of the world ignobly to perish.

If there were and abide certain gains sequent upon
the policy of calculated unfriendliness to the Jew, it
is not less true, alas, that certain obvious injuries
were wrought which affected the fibre of Jewish life.
For one thing, this unhappy relationship evoked a
Jewish self-consciousness, keen and constant, to the
point of morbidness, thus entailing a burden under
the strain of which the less hardy spirits broke

down. But the real hurt done to the Jew by a world which expressed its hostility in a thousand ways— made itself felt in two ways. Of these the one might be named minor and the other major, were it not for the truth that man's spiritual fabric is so finely wrought that even a lesser blow may leave a deadly cancer in its wake.

On the one hand, the antagonism inevitably brought about unworthiness of petty deceit and evasion and wile in the soul of the Jew to adopt the methods of deception and trickery, of unfrankness and indirection, in the world of affairs. But men seldom pause to consider that in a thousand ways the world made it all but imperative for a Jew to resort to stratagem if he would maintain himself at all.

Greater, however, and deeper is the wrong done to the Jew by the world, which removed the caption "No Jews Need Apply" chiefly from the doorpost of church and cathedral, with the result that ofttimes, in other days and in our own day, the Jew, to his shame and the shame of Christendom, chose refuge in the hurtfullest of all evasions, the evasion of desertion, the evasion of apostasy. So true is this that I think of the Jewish tragedy enacted not so much when Jews have been ground down to the dust by the iron heel of an oppressing world as when Jews with shrivelled souls and pitiful rather than contemptible spirits bring themselves to the font of chapel and cathedral, not in token of their quest of renewal of spiritual life, but as a proof that the world without has slain their souls.

If it be true that the contemporaneous resuscitation of the spirit of antagonism raises a grave Jewish problem, it is not less true that it involves an equally grave Christian test. Somehow we will meet and solve the problem as we have not failed to resolve the myriad problems which the centuries have brought to our doors. But can Christendom endure the test?

As it is, Christendom is faced by a most searching test as a result of the war. I am not of the number of those within and without the Christian life who maintain that the war signifies the utter and irretrievable breakdown of Christianity, but I do hold that Christianity, if it is to revive as well as survive, must address itself to the primal task of rooting out of the soul of the millions who dwell within its communion those hatreds which bred the war yesterday, which, if suffered to abide unchallenged, will again and again call forth those antagonisms of the spirit upon which war of necessity follows. The present outburst of hatred and antagonism will not lead to war, civil or international; but as a resolve of the Christian life it shows forth that same disintegration of spiritual fibre which is expressing itself in the outward terms of slaughter and destruction.

If banished this spirit is to be, it will come to pass through those processes of education which not only enlighten the mind and clarify the will, but above all reform and ennoble the purposes of men. But if the change should not come to pass, then will it not be alone morally baleful to Christendom and perhaps even ruinous outwardly to us, but in addition, and perhaps first of all, fatally divisive of the spirit of American life. This was not the perpetuating of a hyphen, but the ruthless use of a jagged-edged cross-cut saw,—forever severing the bond of national life and the common purpose.

The processes of education, if they are to be undertaken by the leaders of Christian life and thought, must go down to the very roots of life, and aim at last and forever to eradicate the deepest-bedded causes instead of furnishing new or furbishing old excuses. The processes of education must end the Christ-killing lie about the Jew and affirm anew the Christ-bearing truth of the Jew in the world. Against every manner of envy and ill-will, of intolerance and unbrotherliness, must the leaders of the Christian life be prepared to do battle.

I ask for nothing less, pleading not in the accents of hopeless beggary but protesting in the spirit of invincible justice, than that in a world calling itself Christian no place be granted to formulae of hatred, of proscription, of bitterness.

The Jew, too, can do much,—from one point of view the Jew can do everything. On the one hand he must avoid giving justification of discrimination, calculated unfriendliness and the spirit of antagonism. On the other hand, and over and above all else, the life of the Jew must be an affirmation of the true, the noble, the holy.

The Jew who offends must remember the truth, however deep be the injustice that underlies, that nine hundred and ninety-nine guiltless Jews will not save the thousandth, but that one guilty Jew suffices to condemn nine hundred and ninety-nine more.

The Jew is adjudged not by the many that are worthy but condemned because of the few that are unworthy.

The Jew is appraised not on the level of his highest and best but of his lowest and meanest.

The noble Jew is hailed as exceptional; the ignoble Jew accepted as typical.

Wo unto the son of the House of Israel who by reason of misdeed adds to the burden borne by all the sons and daughters of his people.

Let the manner and the matter of our life become the crowning proof of the world's injustice to the Jew, so that at last the self-revering dignity, the self-uplifting nobleness of the life of Israel, shall move the world not only to justice to the Jew, but to justice to all the sons of men.

GEORGE GORDON BATTLE

(THE ULTIMATE GOAL)

George Gordon Battle practises law in the City of New York. His ancestors first settled in Virginia in 1689 and later moved to North Carolina, where Mr. Battle was born in 1868. He was educated at the University of North Carolina, was awarded a degree by the University of Virginia in 1889, and received his legal training at Columbia University. But Mr. Battle has been more than active in the practise of law. He has been consistently a progressive in politics and is perhaps best known for his activity in matters of public interest. He gives himself with generous devotion to any cause that is for the betterment of society. He has an extraordinary breadth of relationships throughout the country, and in his own life is an outstanding exponent of the possibility of perfect understanding between peoples of all conditions.

THE ULTIMATE GOAL

BY GEORGE GORDON BATTLE

EX-PRESIDENT COOLIDGE, with character-istic brevity and power of condensation, has packed much thought into these few words—*The demobilisation of post-war racial antagonisms.*

That there was during the period following the Great War an excess of racial antagonism, no one can doubt. Indeed, it could not be otherwise. For four years the world lived in an atmosphere of bitterness and hate. The different races that fought under the flag of the Allies hated those races that followed the standards of the Central Powers. It is true that there was not always harmony even within the boundaries of one nation. In Austria, for instance, the Czechs, the Croats and the Slovaks sympathised rather with their Slavic brethren of Russia and Serbia than with the Magyars of Hungary or the Teutons of Austria. So, too, although the Lithuanians and the Poles were military allies during the early years of the war, there existed between them a racial bitterness al-most as intense as any in Europe. In fact the barriers of race, having their origin in heredity and tradition,

171

were greatly strengthened by the general hostility
and suspicion engendered by the war, which tended
so strongly to make of every man an Ishmaelite in
his feelings toward other races.

After the Armistice this feeling flamed up in many
different manifestations. Lithuania and Poland conducted a private war of their own. The unhappy
Balkan States continued their immemorial custom of
racial hatred and bloodshed. Within the national
boundaries of Russia and Roumania there were pogroms and riots against the Jews. Even here in our
favoured America, we were not free from this feeling.
There was a revival and an accentuation of bigotry
and intolerance of every character. There were race
riots between the whites and the blacks. The stupid
wickedness of the Ku Klux Klan affronted the intelligence and the conscience of the nation. The unfor-
tunate attitude of the Bolshevik government in Russia, with its declared hostility to the economic sys-
tems of all other nations, did much to disturb and
embitter international relations everywhere. The
whole world was full of racial prejudice breaking
out into all manner of excesses—a veritable orgy of
hatreds and post-war passions.

This is no new phenomenon. Every devastating
war has had as its aftermath a similar period. The
Thirty Years War in Germany bred radical antagonisms that exist to the present day. The hatreds

that followed the Napoleonic Wars still curse and divide the countries of the world. The reconstruction period that followed the war between the States produced far more bitterness between the North and the South than had been caused by four years of warfare. And such a result is naturally unavoidable.

Gradually throughout the world these rages and hatreds invoked by war are subsiding. The unexampled devastation and disaster of the war has shocked the conscience of mankind and has alarmed its intelligence. There is undoubtedly a resolution more determined than ever before known in history to prevent the recurrence of a general war. The League of Nations, the World Court, the Disarmament Conferences, the Paris Peace Pact, all show a purpose on the part of the governments of the world to come together, to discuss our national differences, and to attempt to substitute peaceful processes of logic and reason for those of violence and bloodshed. And as we are slowly and painfully striving to settle our international differences, so too in the same gradual and difficult manner we are overcoming the barriers of racial prejudice.

Moreover, there is a distinct tendency toward greater unity of action among the different Churches as evidenced in the coöperation of Catholic, Jew and Protestant in the erection of the great Cathedral of St. John the Divine.

Then, too, in international matters the clashes between Italy and Greece, on the one hand, and Italy and Bulgaria on the other, between Turkey and England, between Roumania and Russia, have all so far been handled through the medium of the League of Nations without war.

Although the millennium is yet far in the future, although men still continue to be greedy and selfish, although the unhappy legacies of racial distrust and dislike still bear down upon us, nevertheless there is throughout the world a disgust for war, a profound conviction that men must overcome these national and racial hatreds if civilisation is to endure, and an eager desire that the burdens of armament be lightened and the world be put upon a basis of peace.

The world is, as I confidently believe, entering upon a phase or an epoch of peace. We can not hope that this progress towards international and inter-racial harmony will be uninterrupted. The line of human development will in the future, as in the past, rise and fall. But, in the future, as in the past, the general course of the line will be upward. And in this forward march of civilisation we look to see the forces of racial prejudice and bigotry and intolerance grow weaker and weaker, as humanity draws nearer towards the ultimate goal of the brotherhood of man.

ISRAEL ABRAHAMS

(THESE LIES WILL NOT LAST)

Israel Abrahams, who died in 1927, *was Reader in Rabbinics at Cambridge University. He had a large part in transplanting from Germany to English-speaking lands the scientific study of Judaism, which in the greatest measure gave impetus to the movement for liberal Judaism in England. Dr. Abrahams was the "Jewish don of Cambridge." Through his personality he succeeded in bringing together Jewish and Christian scholars, and through his erudition Christian and Jewish learning. Dr. Abrahams visited America three times and lectured as a visiting member of the faculty of the Jewish Institute of Religion. Two of these series of lectures have been published by the Alexander Kohut Foundation under the titles "Permanent Values in Judaism" and the "Glory of God." His last work was "Jewish Ethical Wills" in two volumes. Dr. Abrahams, however, will probably best be known for his research studies in the field dealing with the beginnings of Christianity.*

THESE LIES WILL NOT LAST

BY DR. ISRAEL ABRAHAMS

I CAN scarcely persuade myself that the report is accurate. Dr. Sokolow, at the Thirteenth Zionist Congress, said that "the force of anti-Semitism is waning." Contrast this with the annual diatribes of Max Nordau, who depicted anti-Semitism as ever growing in virulence and who almost acclaimed anti-Semitism as an asset—in favor of Zionism. Dr. Sokolow was right. "Anti-Semitism is waning." *It always is waning.*

To understand why this is so it is only necessary to study a tabulation of anti-Semitic lies. H. L. Strack offers such a tabulation. "Secret Societies"? Poor Nilus! The forgery was short-lived, the reaction complete, outside Detroit. The first publishers of the forgery hastened to wash their hands of it when they realised what they had circulated. They threw up the case. They ought never to have fathered it.

This, in brief, is my thesis. Anti-Semitism is recurrent, but it is not continuous; it is intermittent, not cumulative. It changes its note too often for the sound to gather or maintain volume. It is founded

on prejudice and, while prejudice is immortal, prejudices die soon. Before the war Jews were assailed
as capitalists; after the war. as the destroyers of cap-
italist society. There were Jews among the capitalists: there are Jews among the Bolshevists. But the
two charges have slain each other. Most Jews were
found to be poor, their millionaires few. Most Jews
were law-abiding, their Bolshevists exceptional.

These charges will pass—they are passing. For one
Jewish financier there are myriads of Jewish workers
for a daily wage; for one Jewish revolutionary there
are myriads of upholders of social conventions.

Jews will not marry with those not of their creed?
Would it were a true charge! Statisticians prove that
there are more marriages between Jews and Christians than between Protestants and Roman Catholics.
I am sorry. But the fact is a sore blow to certain
types of anti-Semites. And this type knows it. It is
sorry that it spoke. History tells the same story of
other aspects of anti-Semitism.

The myth that the Jews poisoned the wells and
produced the plague of 1348 was countered by the
discovery that Jews were among the worst sufferers,
not only from the ensuing massacres, but from the
black death itself. Harnack, of the first-class authorities, has the distinction of standing alone in his assertion (without a shadow of evidence) that the
Roman Jews instigated the Neronean persecutions of

Christianity. Mommsen's successor in Berlin has scotched this falsehood, once for all.

As for the ritual murder libel it was a bad day for fanatics when the Popes found out that a similar libel had been promulgated by pagans against the early Christians. This particular libel against Jews has been repudiated by hundreds of Christians of the highest academic and ecclesiastical position.

No man who has any self-respect now repeats the charge. All these charges have died, or are dying, an unnatural death. So, too, it is notable that the "international" libel is rapidly failing. So far from getting Jews to pull together in a cosmopolitan spirit, you cannot get them to pull together in local Jewish schemes. Moreover, in presence of the vast numbers of Jews who fought and died for their respective countries in the War, the "international" calumny wears a grotesque garb.

A generation ago it was said that the Jews refused to serve the state, and now we are told that too many Jews fill public positions. The other day a famous English economist himself pointed out to me this contradiction. "I am sure," he said, "that the Jews *gain* by these inconsistent accusations. For when it is realised how inconsistent these false accusations are, the Jews are likely to escape from true criticism." There is much force in this. We Jews might often wonder at the failure of anti-Semites to put their fingers on our real failings. They prefer lies to fair criticism. And *the lies will not last.*

I was rather amused when, the other day, Mr. Chesterton was found rebuking Satan. He protested against the imputation of too much importance to race! Is this champion Aryan turned philo-Semite? At all events Mr. Chesterton sees now that to dub the Jews a separate race—as though such a thing existed as a separate race—is not synonymous with proving them aliens to the common civilisation of the world. Thus all the shibboleths are being silenced. Those who win a passing notoriety, in giving currency to them, pass; the assailed endure. God sitteth in his heaven and laughs.

What's the moral? For the Jews the moral is to answer anti-Semitism by more Semitism, if by Semitism we mean greater devotion to the great ideals which Judaism proclaimed to the world, firmer endeavours to realise those ideals by virtuous persistence in religious and civic well-doing and well-being. For the Christians Strack gave the answer, "The Christian's duty is to maintain veracity and justice." Nay, more: "We must not only refrain from slander and false accusations, but must contradict them in cases where the Jews have difficulty in defending themselves." Strack illustrated his own principle. He died. But *he* has not passed away! Such men speak for all time. The lies do not last. Truth endures.

FRANK GAVIN

(PRIDE AND PREJUDICE)

Frank Gavin is a priest of the Episcopal Church, distinguished by the fact that he followed a course of study in a Jewish theological seminary in preparation for a Professorship of Ecclesiastical History in his own denomination. Dr. Gavin, therefore, understands the problem of Christian-Jewish relations from within, from the study of the literatures of Christianity and Judaism, and from intimate personal contact and experience. He holds degrees from Columbia and Harvard, theological degrees from the General Theological Seminary and the Harvard School of Theology, and from the Hebrew Union College the degree of Habar. He was sometime instructor and Gottheil lecturer at Columbia, Professor of the New Testament at Nashotah Seminary, and is at present Professor of Ecclesiastical History at the General Theological Seminary. His varied learned contributions include studies in the theology of his own church and of the Greek orthodox church, not omitting his latest work on "The Jewish Antecedents of the Sacraments."

PRIDE AND PREJUDICE

BY FRANK GAVIN

SOMETIME ago, in the course of the writer's classroom experience in seminary teaching, he was attempting to trace the various answers to the problem of evil given by the great monotheistic religions. After making a sketch of the Christian doctrine of Original Sin, he attempted to give an objective and sympathetic account of the Rabbinic doctrine of the two *yetzarim*.

One of the students in the class was a priest of the Greek Orthodox Church who, after the lecture, took occasion, in a kind of shame-faced way and with considerable hesitation, to suggest that he found the Rabbinic doctrine infinitely more comprehensible than the Christian one. The same person had frequently ventilated his views on the subject of the Jews, of whom he could in no way approve. Perhaps he may not be classed as an anti-Semite, yet he certainly had no prejudices in favor of anything Jewish. It was, however, highly significant that in the course of his study, when things Jewish came to be presented to him apart from their context, sundered from all that had evil connotation to him, and divorced from what would make them repugnant, this same person was able to evaluate and see certain aspects of Judaism without prejudice or party feeling, objectively and simply. In short, his attitude has a good deal in it that would repay consideration. If you can succeed in denaturing various ideas, you have gone far towards destroying prejudice.

Most of us do not think. Our usual cerebration is what a brilliant speaker once said of a popular reactionary demagogue, whose mental activity he described as "rearranging his prejudices." There is very little in our ordinary life which is not automatic. Past experiences in a large part determine our present responses—from the alarm clock in the morning and our morning tub, throughout the most of the routine activities of the day, to the reflex action of undressing and getting ready for bed, most of our actions are conditioned by our past methods and the monotonous regularity of stimulating incident.

It is not much different with our mental life. We think in grooves. It is so much easier for our minds to come to the same conclusions when a familiar and well-known concept suggests itself than to make a fresh act of mental exertion and isolate the incident as something novel. All our words and terms which have their great significance to us in the connotation they have acquired in the course of our own experience become chiefly meaningful not by reason of their *denotation* so much as by their *connotation*.

Of course, there is something fixed about the meaning or denotation of a word. The same process of fixation takes place about the connotation of a word—and we must be on our guard. When anything always connotes exactly the same experience we are falling into a rut, because we have abandoned the priceless right of self-determination. We are in the way of making our past experience normative and authoritative. Our natural sloth may be depended upon to check the instinct to revise and broaden our range of experience.

This is one great trouble with all the ideas and words (which are only shorthand experience) which have to do with the relations between Jew and non-Jew. An unhappy experience of narrow-minded bigotry or self-assertiveness may attach permanently to the word "Jew" or the word "Gentile" a colourful atmosphere of connotation which will permanently prejudice our judgment.

Ask yourself how largely your views of Gentile or Jew is not a result of a very warped experience plus a very lazy mind. Because three Jews whom I have known were ill-mannered, have I any right to judge in advance what the fourth one will be? Because three Gentiles have been ill-bred, supercilious, suspicious or disdainful, have I the right to conclude in advance that the fourth Gentile I am to meet will follow the rule? It is certainly instinctive to make this kind of mental judgment. It is certainly easy to accumulate this kind of prejudice, but to abandon ourselves to this easy device to escape thinking is to surrender the privilege and power of our personality, and to reduce ourselves permanently to the compass of our own brief and limited past experience.

Most of our prejudices, then, are ready-made reactions developed in advance, and ready prepared for new experience. They foreclose the question. They sterilise the future. They mortgage in advance all the potential possibilities of future knowledge. They warp us, distort us, and twist us into the weird conformation of mind and soul—and, worst of all, they succeed in narcotising us to our very condition. Of course, apart from all consideration of enlightened self-interest, they cripple us for social responsibilities. They lead us to a kind of inbred mental and spiritual character which makes for degeneracy of type.

Prejudices are usually the *sequelae* of a disease called wounded pride. (The word "prejudice" itself has an evil connotation and in that sense it is here used.) I come to dislike that which violates the privileged position I wish for myself, my ideas, or my experience. I cherish my pride, my ideas, and my ex-

perience with a jealous and almost suspicious solici-
tude which resents the slightest aspersion on their
intrinsic superiority.

Most of us (even in a democracy) are not really
democratic. It is instinctively easier to divide our
fellow-men into categories of inferior and superior
than to maintain with a steady consistency of outlook that we are all essentially equals. Even a democracy helps on our instincts, because it allows us
for the most part to choose our own superiors, and
the rest of mankind we can lump as inferiors. It is
the hardest thing for us to make real to ourselves the
actuality of the democratic attitude, to keep from
either the valleys or the mountain peaks of mental
position, and to stand on the same level with our
fellows. It is just our prejudices which are fundamentally useful to us in protecting or safeguarding
a position of mental or moral superiority; our prejudices reinstate us where we would like to be, and
reduce others to the position in which we would have
them be.

So the most important task before us is a job of
mental house cleaning. It is the enormous increment,
increasing day by day, of limited experience and
foregone conclusions which hampers wholesome
mental and social activity. We ought not to wait,
until we are compelled to clean house by some catastrophe or emergency, to examine objectively and

clearly the results of our partial experiences in the past. There are some kinds of possessions which are a burden, and prejudices based on inadequate data certainly belong to this class.

Hillel's and Jesus' versions of the Golden Rule are a pretty good guide for us in the process of dry-cleaning our mental impedimenta. So many of the factors in our prejudices cancel each other off. The Jew so often dislikes the Gentile for the very same reason the Gentile dislikes the Jew. Is it not ridiculous that sane folk of the twentieth century should refuse to grow up into that breadth of outlook in social relations, the possession of which in so many other relations of living we continually affirm? For every Gentile whose experience with Jews has been disheartening and unhappy, there is at least one Jew whose experience with Gentiles has been identical. Is it not irrational to impute to a class or a type or an aggregation the failings of an individual? Is not that precisely what Jews and Gentiles do in relation to one another?

Let us dispose once for all of any "religious issue" in the whole matter. True Judaism is no more anti-Christian than true Christianity is anti-Jewish. No more warrant can be found in Hillel's than in Jesus' teaching for antagonism or hatred. Any Jew who falls back on his religion to vindicate his prejudice against Christians is as disloyal and unfaithful a

Jew as the Christian, who does likewise, is a disloyal and unfaithful Christian.

Christian creeds have forever stigmatised a non-Jew as the agent whereby Jesus' death was accomplished: "Suffered under Pontius Pilate, was crucified, dead, and buried." There is no mention of Jews, no tinge of anti-Judaism. No Christian can add to his creeds without doing despite to the historic formulations of his faith. The excoriation of the Pharisees in Saint Matthew's Gospel (perhaps the most apparently anti-Jewish portion of the New Testament) can be matched equally, or even outdone, by the denouncements of false Pharisees in the Talmud. There is no religious ground for anti-Jewish or anti-Christian prejudices.

The greatest cause and the most generous explanation of the seemingly age-long prejudices between Jew and non-Jew is ignorance. Ignorance cannot be dispelled by information solely. Deep down in most of us are substrata of presuppositions and prejudgments which must be excavated out, scrutinised, and removed before we will be able to allow plain facts to gain admittance. Good-will must be gained before information can be received .

The whole crux of the problem of education, as the only means of dispelling prejudices, rests in the task of gaining good-will. That it is a "good heart," which is the priceless possession, is the teaching of the Rabbis and Jesus. We need a steady growth in sympathy and intelligence before we can eradicate the evil.

Every Jew has no less a duty than every Christian. It is the tone of voice which expresses one's temper of mind. One's temper or attitude is creative; we see, for the most part, what we want to see in our fellow-men. It is only by taking as a standard for our "prejudices" what our knowledge and thinking can give us as the best norm of Christian and best standard of Jew, that we can ever build a solid foundation of peace and good-will.

Every time we let loose on society, no matter in how intimate a circle, the ventilation of our pent-up feeling of prejudice and the expression of the sense of wrong, against the Jews if we are non-Jews, and against non-Jews if we are Jews, we are doing our best to perpetuate an atmosphere of suspicion and hostility which it is our bounden duty to dissipate. It is fundamentally wrong-headedness which makes the exception not prove the rule so much as illustrate it.

We must begin by taking steps forward toward the pledging of ourselves to the great end of peace and freedom; freedom, to be deliberately purchased at the price of neutralising prejudice and fallen pride, and peace, as the fruit of this victory. Let us dedicate ourselves, non-Jew and Jew, to this end.

JONAH B. WISE

(RELIGION : THE COMMON DENOMINATOR)

Jonah B. Wise is the son of Isaac Mayer Wise, the most striking personality in American Jewish history; but Jonah B. Wise travels on his own momentum as a forceful character in the American rabbinate. Educated both in the United States and abroad, he built up a significant ministry in Oregon and the Pacific Coast as the successor of Stephen S. Wise in Congregation Beth Israel of Portland. There he was prominent not only in local and state educational projects, but was an active servant of the state in important public problems and a mediator in local disputes. In 1925 he accepted the call to the Central Synagogue in New York City. While on the Coast he was the editor of the Jewish publication, "The Scribe," and in 1928 he took over the editorship of the "American Israelite" which was founded by his father 75 years ago.

RELIGION : THE COMMON DENOMINATOR

BY JONAH B. WISE

THE expression of religion in mathematical terms is unfair. Still, one might be excused if one borrowed the exact terminology of the most exact of sciences to describe part of the most exacting of experiences. Religion makes enormous demands. It makes them on more people than any other social factor; it sets a greater task for the individual and the mass. It makes more loyalties and more inherited affiliations than any art, science or political experience of the human race. It functions equally amongst cultured and crude, civilised and savage, white, black, brown and yellow. When men meet they may find few experiences common to all which establish a contact, hostile, friendly or neutral; but religion offers such a meeting place.

Religion is, has been, and will continue to be, a common experience for all people, positively or negatively, actively or inactively, touching every life somewhere, somehow. No door leading to human effort has ever been successfully closed to it.

It has changed because it has touched the arts, the sciences and the policies of human society. Where it did not originate it profoundly influenced, and where it did not destroy, it radically altered. For evil or for good, religion has coloured every phase of human endeavour. This is true among the most as well as the less and least enlightened. Its influence is as significant and as certain in an enlightened English or American gathering as it is in a Coolie meeting or a Hottentot conclave. In fact, religion is so subtle an element in human society that it functions more forcefully when freed in a more aspiring culture than it does when confined in a less enlightened one.

Josiah Royce says, "A man's religious faith, whatever more special items of doctrine it may involve, means for me essentially his faith in the existence of an unseen order of some kind in which the riddles of the natural order may be explained."

All religions are, at bottom, one, in their origins in man's native tendency to a more buoyant interpretation of himself in his world. The gross as well as the refined find an inspiration or a challenge to a better adjustment to life in religion. It is, therefore, the one experience known to all ages, all types and all circumstances, and is in itself the great common denominator of man's life.

A pressing necessity of our age is to find a universal fact, some common factor, which will establish a

conscious kinship between men. Religion has had a
hectic and tumultuous career. It has united groups
with a power inherent in no other social phenomenon. The Koran and the sword of the prophet transformed an anarchic crowd of Yemenite Bedouins into a world conquering unity; the assumption of the
symbol of the cross and the idea of rescuing the
Holy Sepulchre made for a union of European
peoples, staggering in its firmness and theretofore
impossible and unthinkable.

There is no part of the world, no section of human history, that has not found in religion a means
for securing what was wanted or needed, things for
which the common powers of men were often inadequate. The early settlement of America has a conscious religious background reflected in every colonial
group, and recognised by Burke in his speech on "The
Conciliation of the American Colonies."

A curious tribute to this inevitable background to
human history is the following: Bishop Agostino
Guistiniano of a patrician family of Genoa, com-
mentating in an Italian 1516 edition of the Psalms
in Hebrew, on Psalm 19, verse 6, "His line goeth out
to the ends of the earth," says, "In our own times,
by his wonderful daring, Christopher Columbus, the
Genoese, has discovered almost another world and a
new congregation of Christians. In truth, as Columbus often maintained that God had chosen him as

the instrument for the fulfillment of this prophecy, I deem it not improper here to refer to his life." (David Amram's translation.) Lincoln's reference to the same Psalm in his Second Inaugural Address in the use of the words, "The judgments of the Lord are true and righteous altogether," carries the thread of religious potency from Genoa to Washington, from a Bishop barely escaped from mediævelism to the free mentality of the great emancipator.

Great accomplishments by masses of humanity must be motivated by profound impulses. Trivial forces have no place in history. Where a great need arises, a great power must be employed. Despite all his intellectual possibilities, man is a clumsy and fumbling creature. He has succeeded only at a cost which is often ridiculously out of proportion in effort to the end attained.

To-day he has consciously or unconsciously set as an objective the attainment of peace between men and nations. The latter are more difficult to hold in check than the former. International relations are grotesquely old fashioned and childish. Napoleon tried to create a means of contact between states which was direct and candid. His failure to do so was his real Waterloo. Our Balkanised international relations are the result of archaic terms in the hands of hopeless valetudinarians. As between men, an establishment of a better order is potentially within the power of a greater and more intelligent force.

The Prophet Micah once wrote about a universal force which would bring peace to men. He believed that it was religion but, curiously enough, not necessarily his religion, for he says (Micah 4:1-5)—

"But in the last days it shall come to pass, that the mountain of the house of the Lord shall be established in the top of the hills; and people shall flow unto it.

"And many nations shall come, and say: Come, and let us go up to the mountain of the Lord, and to the house of the God of Jacob; and He will teach us of His ways, and we will walk in His paths: for the law shall go forth out of Zion, and the word of the Lord from Jerusalem.

"And He shall judge between many peoples and rebuke strong nations afar off; and they shall beat their swords into ploughshares, and their spears into pruning hooks; nation shall not lift up sword against nation, neither shall they learn war any more.

"But they shall sit every man under his vine and under his fig tree; and none shall make them afraid: for the mouth of the Lord of hosts hath spoken it.

"For all people will walk every one in the name of his god, and we will walk in the name of the Lord our God for ever and ever."

Micah was a liberal. He claims that the essential corollary to his peace pact is to "walk every one in the name of his god." Here is to be found the key to the use of religion as a factor for good-will. Strange that it should have been so well stated such a long time ago, and so little used even in our day! One cannot escape the logic of it. Religion is a barrier to human unity which is insurmountable when it permits its motives and methods to shrink to the level of other partisan programs. The selfish salvationism which produced an inquisition is a type of religious littleness not peculiar to Rome, but common to all sects which demand a monopoly of the right to chaperone humanity into heaven. Such thinking has seared men's bodies to save their souls.

The question naturally arises as to whether the religions of men can ever be big enough to render the service demanded to-day, or whether they will continue in the light of cultural democracy to shrink more and more into cruel and warring sects. One cannot dismiss religion. Its most discouraged ministers and most disillusioned votaries must finally come to that conclusion. One can and must utilise it. To do so it must be liberal. That is the first step.

What is Liberal Religion? One might say without irreverence, "The Lord only knows." Is it a revolt against forms and customs? Not at all. Those things are mere incidents and the dislike of them can hardly

be sufficient cause for intelligent opposition. Is it
rebellion against priests, prelates, pastors and pres-
byters? Not at all. They are the human machinery,
despite the claims, and dissent from their authority is
not the basis for a positive movement. Is it disagree-
ment with dogma? Not entirely. Dogma and convictions are often miles apart. A dead dogma or a distasteful one will disappear of itself.

Liberal religion is the democratisation of faith. It
is the high spiritual achievement of our day. It is not
a cheap alloy of concessions, quarrels and emenda-
tions. It is the natural result of actual, vital religious
experience. A liberal in faith can conceivably be a
pope, a Methodist bishop or a country vicar. For to
be such he need not concede the validity of another
sect's ideas, but its right under God to have them.
That doctrine has been fought for with blood and
tears for centuries. It is, however, basic to religion's
place as the common denominator in human good-
will, and until it is accepted in principle there can be
no such thing. Liberal religion is the recognition of
the inherent right of every man to "walk, every one
in the name of his god." From that standpoint there
can conceivably come a service which faith is capable
of rendering, in that it will unite men while retaining
for each its own best powers.

There will never be a universal religion in the
sense that there will be no sects. It is not only impos-

sible, it is undesirable. Man interprets himself best by groupings which are naturally different. Life is a game. One of its reasons and helps is the interplay of healthful rivalries. While one cannot foresee the time when religions will be sportsmanlike, one can predict the day when they will be mutually tolerant.

The serious clash of religious experiences will vitalise life. It will release energies which it alone has in the past been able to command. They exhibited themselves in crusades, in missions to unexplored regions; in ministrations to the sick, the poor and the disinherited. It has done tremendous things.

Liberal religion takes religion seriously. It is unwilling to give it up because of the criticisms mentioned before. It believes in this eternal reaction of man to his environment and God. The things which divide men and parties are the little ones. Gulliver's Lilliputians warred over opening an egg at the big or little end. The animosities and jealousies of life arising from rivalries in business, love and ambition are endless and inevitable. The palliatives for these are not to be found in them. A greater and a nobler than they must intercede, and that better or even best in human affairs is undeniably religion, but only religion raised to its best powers. It is hopeful that all will eventually concede that freedom to all which will make for good-will between men, with faith as the common denominator.

WALTER PRICHARD EATON

(DRAMA: A BOND OF FELLOWSHIP)

Walter Prichard Eaton is perhaps the dean of American dramatic critics—certainly among those who keep abreast of the developments made by our native drama. His outspokenness was detrimental to the advertising columns and is said to have lost him at least one lucrative position, but that same episode gained him a host of followers. He has reviewed with equal authority both plays and music. For the past two decades he has been virtually a free lance, but all the more ardent in his efforts to contribute creatively to the development of American playwriting. The little theatre movement owes much of its virility and fine promise to the encouragement received at the hands of Mr. Eaton. His essays and books on the subject have stimulated almost national response to this wholesome movement in America—and in Europe, too. A keen lover of Nature, Mr. Eaton has written extensively, in a lucid style and with an outlook infectiously optimistic, on the allure of the beckoning outdoors.

DRAMA: A BOND OF FELLOWSHIP

BY WALTER PRICHARD EATON

THE world is seeking, as perhaps never before, for agencies to break down the barriers of misunderstanding between nations, and between races. What share has the theatre played in breaking down such barriers? What share can it play? At first glance, its share might seem great, because the theatre is so nearly universal in its appeal. But has it fulfilled this natural expectation?

In our understanding of the ancient Greeks to-day we get enormous help from the comparatively few dramas which have come down to us, and in a revival of one of these plays, in a classic amphitheatre, we come as close, perhaps, as it is possible to come to the life of Athens. But when we in New York perform a play from modern France or Russia, do we gain thereby a clearer understanding of those people, and by that understanding decrease the likelihood of future trouble with them, of bigotry and intolerance? We strive historically to understand a dead people, through their imperishable drama. Do we equally strive to understand a living people through their current drama, or do we accept it merely as entertainment, as we might buy their laces or pressed dates at a shop?

When I first began to go to the theatre more than thirty years ago, I should say that there was still very little effort on anybody's part to understand another race or nation from its acted drama, and that translated (and generally freely "adapted") plays had little more than a simple entertainment value. Augustin Daly adapted sentimental and farcical German plays with no other thought than giving his actors "fat parts" to gambol in. Authors still stole right and left from the French stage, as they had been doing for the past fifty years, because the French built better dramatic frameworks then, and also because the Gallic source permitted a touch of the risque, so frowned upon, and enjoyed, by the Anglo-Saxon. On the whole, this process probably made for a still too prevalent misunderstanding of France and the French. The profoundly serious dramas of Ibsen, which couldn't very well be tampered with (though Modjeska gave *The Doll's House* a happy ending!), were at first greeted with cries of outrage and horror, and tended to immerse us still further in our belief that the Atlantic mercifully separated us from the "cesspool of Europe"— a term actually used by one New York critic. The old German street bands of my youth were much more ambassadors of international good-will than were the foreign plays.

All this has been radically changed in my own adult lifetime, and I'm inclined to think it one of the most significant changes in our theatre. It came about, of course, directly as a result of international copyright and the increased respect of theatre artists for the integrity of a fellow artist's work. There was no conscious social purpose in it. Copyright made it impossible (or at least dangerous) to steal from a foreign dramatist and adapt his play out of all recognition; and increased artistic consciousness made actors, authors and even audiences aware that the value of any work lies in its truth to its own time and place—that Ibsen isn't Ibsen unless faithfully translated, nor *The Weavers* of the slightest value unless the spirit of social revolt and that noble mass emotion are rendered. But whatever the causes, the result now is that all our better producers and authors seek more or less faithfully to render the true spirit of foreign work, that we now even seek the skilled foreign interpreters to give us the original, direct, and that we look for the racial and national differences in drama, as well as the universal likenesses, relish them, consciously gain understanding from them.

This is, after all, a very considerable change in the brief space of a generation.

Take, for example, such a play as *The Cherry Orchard* or *The Three Sisters*. In my youth Tchekhov could not possibly have been translated and understood in America, and not merely because we had heard less about Russia then. We were not trained then, even in our own drama, to the finer and subtler representations of national character, and especially we never looked for such truth in translations. An exact rendering of *The Cherry Orchard* would have hopelessly bewildered us. But to-day we accept it as a supreme naturalistic study of Russian character in Tchekhov's generation, and from it we gain not only the pleasure of subtle art, but added understanding of another race, which may not clarify for us all that takes place in Moscow, but at least enables us to look at it as something with roots in a different soil from ours, and hence not yielding to our snap judgments.

Within our own nation, I have often wondered if the negro minstrels, which began in the 1840's, didn't perhaps play a larger part in the Civil War than has ever been exploited. It is difficult to imagine those troupes of "black face" comedians, getting their music, dances and much of their simple humour from negro sources, not greatly increasing the national sympathy for the black race. At any rate, in our own day, the opening of a clear window into the life of a dusky, alien race to reveal its surging,

unconscious life, as in *Porgy*, or the eloquent
revelation of the tragedy between ambition and
power of accomplishment, as in Paul Green's *In
Abraham's Bosom*, have unquestionably aided in an
understanding of the negro and in sympathy and
tolerance. Even from so second-rate a drama as
Abie's Irish Rose, full of claptrap and "hokum"
and totally unindividualised stock characters, thousands of beholders, by their own testimony, got a
kind of warm, sentimental glow of tolerance. Sometimes it may have been, no doubt, perilously akin to
the emotional glow of a religious "revival," which
doesn't translate itself into action and is gone the
next day. We are told that emotions which are not
translated into action are not of much value, such as
those of the Russian lady mentioned by William
James, who wept with pity at a play while her coach-
man froze to death outside. Nevertheless, a glow of
tolerance once roused is never quite forgotten. It is,
at least, easier to arouse it a second time.

Certainly the glow of indignation at the English
penal system roused by Galsworthy's *Justice* was
translated into some action in England—or so we
have been told. Certainly the intellectual glow at
Shaw's *Arms and the Man*, first of his plays dis-
closed to us, by Richard Mansfield, back in the '90's
continued to aid in the ferment of modern ideas, and
the revaluation of many old values. Certainly the

Robots of the Capeks' play, *R. U. R.* (a term for
a mechanical man which has now even appeared in
the international sporting news) have caused thousands to think more seriously upon the problems and
destiny of our new machine civilisation, and their
influence has not ceased with the falling curtain.

If, then, plays can, and do, have influence in
shaping the thought and consciousness of their own
nations, or their own day when they deal with universal themes, as war in *Arms and the Man* and
machine society in *R. U. R.*, is it not logical to
suppose that the next step is for them to have influence in the relations between races and nations?
Is it not pretty certain that if they are exchanged,
in their integrity, they already must have such an
effect? Is not the question of what plays are exchanged, then, rather more important than we may
have supposed, and perhaps too much left to chance
and the merely commercial instinct?

I have in mind especially the present situation between England and the United States. England since
the War seems to be shy on dramatists who can provide the popular fare essential to keeping theatres
open in an era of high rentals and inflated costs. The
managers have turned to the United States for aid
(it used to be the other way around), and are importing our "best seller" type of play by the dozen.
Critics like St. John Ervine complain of this, seem-

ing to blame us for it, which is quite unjust, but also pointing out that these plays, with their crooks and gunmen and "hoofers," give an unfair and distorted idea of the United States, which is no doubt true enough. As a matter of fact, the "best seller" type of play, in any nation, gives a distorted picture of that nation. Yet it is always the type of play first seized upon for translation or use elsewhere, because it represents the kind of exciting story or romantic sentimentality easily understood and relished by the masses of every race.

But by a curious human limitation, while we unconsciously discount the romantic sentimentality and the distorted pictures in plays of our own, we think the same sort of plays from abroad are a true picture. No American believed his country entirely composed of crooks, however much he enjoyed the epidemic of crook dramas. But for years the average American judged France by the Palais Royal farces and was sure every Frenchman kept as many mistresses as he could afford, and no French woman was virtuous unless ugly. So we found British critics complaining of the "American invasion" of the London stage, because it caused Englishmen to fancy America a land of crooks, bootleggers, demi-reps, and unsavoury characters of all sorts, and to scorn us accordingly.

All this shows with unmistakable clearness the superior value of first rate art, and the fundamental unsoundness of those well meaning efforts of "good" people to discourage serious, realistic art in favor of sentimentalism. The type of person who advocates censorship, for instance, or who says, "There's enough unhappiness in the world without reading about it," and who accordingly admires Gene Stratton Porter's books but is shocked by Ibsen or O'Neill, joins a kind of conspiracy to falsify the nations to each other and to make more difficult mutual understanding. *It is not only the fine, serious, imaginative works of any race which best explain it to another race, it is also the works which criticise the race from within, which dissect and even flay it.* We don't think less of the English because Shaw laughs at them; we may accept his criticism, but because the English let him criticise and laugh with him, we get a new insight into their fundamental love of free speech, which is often so much deeper than ours, and salted with more humour.

We have always looked to England for some of our finest stage works, and dramatists like Pinero, Jones, Shaw, Barrie and Galsworthy have probably enjoyed as great, if not greater, success in America as at home. The fine seriousness of purpose, or the wit, or the style, or the charm of such works have never permitted us to underestimate our British cousins, and have given us in a thousand ways a better understanding of British character and British problems.

It is certainly no more than fair, then, that England, when importing our plays, should import some of our best along with the popular "crook" and "mystery" melodramas. They should judge us by the brooding, poetic passion of O'Neill, the clear-cut workmanship of Sydney Howard, the wholesome homely truth of Frank Craven, the satiric realism of George Kaufmann, the polished style of Philip Barry. If they make no effort to import our best plays, it is their fault if they fail to understand America.

O'Neill, for example, is not at all a typical American dramatist, in the sense that his style and his characters conform to the popular standard, and fit the popular mold. But in the sense that he has reached, through our theatre, a high pitch of imaginative power and represents our dramatic expression in its finest flower of matured art, he is *the* typical American dramatist. A foreign nation, hearing his plays in their integrity, can no longer consider us artistic barbarians, in spite of our Hollywood horrors, but is bound to gain some respect for us, to think of us as imaginatively mature—at least in spots.

To the ancient Greeks anybody not a Greek was a barbarian. It is, alas! only too common to-day to find that attitude in every race, toward all the others. If Americans are less inclined to look upon the

English as barbarians than upon other races, that is not alone because we speak the same language, but because we have so long realised at first hand the glories of English literature and bowed in enforced humbleness before British dramas. England will think of us less as ignorant, bumptious little country cousins when they have seen the best instead of the worst of our plays. And we shall think far more of Russia and Germany and other peoples of alien race or tongue when we have seen more of their drama, in its integrity. The Moscow Art Theatre, Reinhardt's troupe, Hungarian plays like *Liliom*, all the more or less recent importations to America of first rate plays and productions of the world theatre, have not only lifted the standards of the American theatre, but have made most Americans directly exposed to them far more respectful of foreign peoples, far more inclined to exchange art instead of bullets and contempt.

The misunderstanding and contempt for "foreigners" is to-day far more prevalent in those regions where the new theatre and world literature do not penetrate. That alone ought to show us that to further the penetration of international art, presented in its integrity, undoctored to meet popular romantic taste, is to further directly and effectively the cause of international understanding and good-will.

GEORGE S. HELLMAN

(ART: A UNIVERSAL LANGUAGE)

George S. Hellman, poet, essayist, educator and art critic, sees humanity with mellow vision and approaches the subject of art from the angle of its universal appeal. Mr. Hellman began his literary career early in his college days. He is distinguished especially as the one who rescued from probable oblivion numerous unpublished literary ana of Robert Louis Stevenson and Washington Irving. Very few were given the opportunity to know the rank and file that was afforded Mr. Hellman during the post-war educational endeavours made for the American enlisted men in France immediately after the Armistice. The French Government recognised this service by conferring upon him the order of Officier d' Academie. His revealing biography, "Washington Irving, Esquire," is of enduring merit, and many an otherwise untold anecdote sparkles in his "Lanes of Memory."

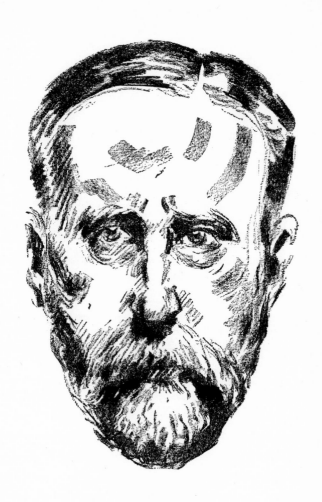

ART: A UNIVERSAL LANGUAGE

BY GEORGE S. HELLMAN

IN considering the significance of Art in world
relations, we are called upon to ponder the im-
ponderable; to weigh values for which there are no
adequate scales. But it is the values that have weight,
not the scales, and every intelligent man is aware
that on the life of the spirit rests the ultimate
vitality of human progress.

Now Art, in the sense that it is most commonly
accepted, is the channel through which human emotions flow in some form of harmony, observable to
the sight or hearing of the world of men. Pursuing
this metaphor, we may look upon all human activities as fields accessible to the beneficent waters
that stream through the channel of Art. Yet in all
the centuries of modern civilisation no concerted
attempt has been made on the part of nations to re-
construct Society on the basis of man's reaction to
all those impulses which are the impulses of beauty.

If we concede for the moment, or rather if we
accept without discussion as incontestable, the physi-

cal necessities of mankind—the need of food, of shelter, the need of health and of cleanliness, the needs of sex—we arrive at the yearning towards beauty as a non-physical basis of unity among men. When we speak of Art as the one universal language, we are not indulging in rhetoric; we are involved in a profound truth.

Consider how in studying past history, we record with prejudice of aversion, with prejudice of partisanship, the political, the economic, the scientific, even the religious struggles of bygone ages. Alone in the domain of beauty do we meet as brothers; and alone Art, among the works of man, bridges the chasm between the past and future.

Why is it that when the Germans hurled their projectiles at the Cathedral of Rheims the soul of mankind shuddered? Had they destroyed innumerable insignificant church buildings, there would'have been no protest. The indignation aroused was not an indignation due to an affront against any religious edifice *per se*, but the attack on Rheims Cathedral was recognised, even by those who could not analyse their emotions, as an insult to the order of things, an act of sacrilege committed against a glorious symbol of that spirituality wherein all men meet in their reaction towards beauty.

Love of beauty is innate in every human being. The impulse towards Art is expressed by every individual and by every nation in its infancy. The child draws before he can speak, and the tribe engraves on wood and stone long before it frames the tribal laws. There is no person, however restricted by circumstances or poverty, or by lack of rudimentary education, who does not react in some way towards beauty. Indeed, poverty does not prevent the creation of beauty, as the thirteenth century in France bears witness. It does interfere with the far-spread appreciation of beauty because this appreciation is not widely possible in any age wherein materialism creates economic slaves. The enjoyment of beauty, which is a natural right of every man, is thus interwoven with the entire civilised advance. Now that America, in especial, has arrived at a stage of economic development where the population as a whole has increasing leisure, it would seem to behoove us to take the leadership in the cultivation of the values associated with Art—and in Art one includes, of course, not only painting and sculpture and architecture, but also music and poetry; all the fields wherein the voice of beauty sings.

When we approach the theme specifically from its international aspect, we begin with the obvious yet profound fact that better international relations depend on better international understanding. Nations will always remain rivals, and in the realm of commercial wealth and the power that results from com-

mercial wealth, such rivalry will never be wholly
free from the seeds of antagonism. This does not obtain in the rivalry of Art, and the artist is the true
ambassador of good-will. He is this for many reasons. He is this, first of all, because what he creates
is a common asset of humanity. He gives to all nations without taking away from any, and at the
same time he increases the stature of his own country
in the eyes of all other countries. Velasquez and
Goya have done more for the glory of Spain than all
its politicians have been able to accomplish; Poe and
Whitman have in France done more for America
even than Benjamin Franklin; Washington Irving
was the first to cause the European people to think
of the United States as a country not wholly crude
and negligible; hardly had the Armistice been
signed, the Great War ended, when the music of
Beethoven was again heard in Paris. And if the artist
is the proponent of good-will because he contributes
to the higher joys of all peoples, he is equipped for
his international task by virtue of his temperamental
philosophy, as well as by reason of his talent. He
is essentially the philosopher despite the emotional-
ism which is a necessity of his being. The musician,
the poet, the painter, knows that the finest things of
life are far removed from the mean competition of
commercial affairs and that the continuity of the
race-life is based on the spiritual oneness in man's

nature, on those passions and aspirations in which past, present and future are linked.

While the physical urge to create would seem to assure the permanence of the human race, it is the spiritual urge to enjoy creations of beauty that makes for the progress of mankind, if there is to be any high progress. I wonder if we Americans realise how widespread and how deep amongst ourselves is this spiritual urge to create and enjoy beauty. Some of us who, during the six months that elapsed between the signing of the Armistice and the return of the American troops, had charge of the instruction of the American Expeditionary Forces in the field of Art, had occasion to learn that the youth of America was amazingly eager—out of all proportion, as we thought, eager—to study and to appreciate Art. Thousands upon thousands of soldiers applied for the courses in architecture, in painting, in sculpture and commercial design. And we learned also, in practical fashion, that love of Art was a cement among nations, for we saw the interest of France in the art work of the American soldiers. The Art school at Fontainebleau, established by the French government, where young Americans now go every year to study, is a development of the experiment conducted by the American Army, and one may be well assured that when these Americans return to their own country they will come back as friends of France.

What France is doing at Fontainebleau, all nations should do, but on an even wider scale. Men of great wealth and all leaders of thought who are interested in developing better understanding among nations should turn their minds to what Art, which has no frontiers, which breaks down barriers and which makes for the democracy of the spirit, can effect along the lines of such increased amity. But in order to accomplish this aim most effectively, the first necessity is for men of wealth to realise that it is far more important to encourage the work of living artists than to collect masterpieces of the dead. When an American millionaire buys at a great price an European masterpiece, he will, in some instances, be a party to the violation of some national law. In all instances he is adding to that irritation against our preponderant wealth which is one of the main sores on the body of nations. The masterpieces of the European countries, whether these works of Art are indigenous or have for centuries been in the national possession, are part of the nation's heritage and traditions.

But if the American millionaire purchases the painting of, say, a living French artist or finances the education of a living German composer, he will pay an appreciable compliment to Europe and he will become a constructive force in the present-day life of the nation whose artist he is encouraging. He will not meet with the implicit rebuke that fell to the lot of the American who paid a fortune for an old French tapestry only to have France forbid its export. He will not have the foreign press expostulating against the weight of the dollar, which often breaks into real values while creating fictitious values. Of course, there can be no question concerning the immediate right of any man to use his wealth for any legitimate purposes that give him personal pleasure. But we are considering now what the far-minded citizen of the world can do to' bring into more sympathetic understanding the citizenry of all nations.

What if Mr. X., who during the past few years is said to have spent $5,000,000 on old masterpieces, and very lovely pictures they unquestionably are, had placed his millions at the disposal of the American government for an experiment that has never been tried? What if he had said: "I should be glad to have the nation invite a group of creators of beauty—painters, poets, architects, musicians, sculptors—to come for one year to our country; to work here; to have at least some closer idea of our ways and thoughts. In this group there should be, say, one hundred men and women: ten nations of Europe. South America and Asia shall be represented. Ten artists from each country. They are each to receive $5,000 for their maintenance during their stay in

America, and I am willing to continue this expenditure for ten years."

If Mr. X. had done this, we should have a thousand creators of beauty as the emissaries of good-will towards America on the continents. We are, as I have said at the beginning, in the realm of imponderables; but can anyone doubt that this one man would have made a greater contribution to international relations, a greater contribution on the constructive side of beauty itself, than his collection of the works of dead artists can ever accomplish? And if one man might have done this, think what the wealth of America can do, if our millionaires become a little less selfish, a little less snobbish, a great deal more adventuresome in their interest. And as a corollary to some such plan, a plan which could be similarly carried out on a less munificent scale in other lands, there might spring up in the capitals of each country museums devoted to foreign Art.

It is too much to hope that war among peoples will soon cease, so deep-rooted are the misrepresentations and the rivalries which separate and antagonise the various nations of the world; but it is not too soon to realise that as the appreciation of beauty in the scheme of existence grows among mankind, war itself will become more and more remote.

GEORGE W. OCHS-OAKES

(LETTERS: INTERNATIONAL CEMENT)

George Washington Ochs-Oakes was born at Cincinnati in 1861 while his father was fighting the rebels, hence the patriotic cognomen expressive of his sire's intense patriotism. He drifted down to Chattanooga with his family after the war and there was twice elected Mayor of the town. Coming north in 1901, he became editor and publisher of the Philadelphia Times and the Philadelphia Ledger; and in 1915, editor and general manager of the Current History Magazine of the New York Times. Mr. Oakes likes to recall that he boxed the compass on the Chattanooga Times, occupying every position from reporter to editor-in-chief and publisher. The French Government decorated him with a Cross of the Legion of Honour after publishing the Paris Exposition daily edition of the New York Times. Mr. Oakes is president of the Chattanooga Society of New York. He is an authority on history-in-the-making, and under his régime the dignified magazine over which he presides has won merited prestige.

LETTERS: INTERNATIONAL CEMENT

BY GEORGE W. OCHS-OAKES

THE forces of imperialism, nationalism, territorial ambition, commercial rivalry and racial hatreds had been threatening civilisation for several decades. They fell like a thunderbolt in 1914. The storm which followed raged with unparalleled fury while it lasted. When the rays of peace again kissed the earth—fitful at first, growing more radiant day by day—it left a cleansed and clearer atmosphere, as does a storm in Nature which has spent itself.

True, many profound problems of delicate character are yet unsolved; many waste places are yet to be restored. But survey the world to-day, by and large, and you must perceive the promise of a firmer, more stable, more peaceful outlook than has ever before existed among the children of men.

Everywhere one turns there is discernible a movement which has for its goal international amity and understanding. The whole world is sick of war and its frightful havoc. Turn to the chancelleries of all the Powers and we find the statesmen everywhere committed to some form of action which looks to closer affiliation. They may differ as to methods, they may each have a separate plan, yet all are striving to reach the common end of closer understanding, each according to his own lights.

In another direction, invincible forces are moving toward world understanding and fraternity which are even more powerful in their reactions than the manifestations in the realm of politics and economics—a world-wide cultural coöperation—the cementing of international friendships through alliances in art, literature and education.

It has been well said that international understandings and friendships cannot be established by mere edicts, nor can they be developed solely by popular desire, if the instrumentalities are lacking to execute the popular will. The converse is equally true: that the most perfect machinery of international intercourse cannot function unless it has, as its propelling force, the irresistible power of public opinion or popular good-will. This cannot be obtained by pious declarations, executive mandates or legislative enactments. It is a process of growth, of development. The seed must be sown skillfully; it must be carefully nurtured and cultivated in soil enriched by husbandmen who understand its nature. In other words, to change the simile, to reach the people and implant in their souls the will to world fraternity, requires a process of education and enlightenment, the encouragement to free contacts with their fellow-men of different races and nationalities.

Each new access of literary, artistic or enlightening achievement in the world's history is traceable to the influence of new contacts. What is true in culture is likewise equally true in politics and economics. The French Revolution saw its repercussion throughout the world; the industrial revolution in England was followed by similar phenomena in every land. The contacts of European civilisation with alien peoples through the Colonial expansion of the fifteenth and sixteenth centuries completely transformed the political, social, literary and scientific life of Europe.

What was true then will inevitably follow in a larger sense to-day, with our increased means of communication and our enlarged facilities for active, instantaneous intercourse. Hence the development of international education, as reflected in the great International University at Brussels, justifies the conviction that we are at the threshold of a new era in civilisation.

Other notable activities looking to international universities are in progress. The Institute of Politics at Williams College brings to its round table discussions many of the most illustrious intellectuals and statesmen of the world. At Chicago the Norman Waite Harris Foundation "for the promotion of a better understanding on the part of American citizens of the other peoples of the world" is in successful operation, and another, the Furman Institute in South Carolina, is successfully proceeding on similar lines. Recently there was established at Johns Hopkins University the Walter Hines Page School of International Relations under the direction of a group of our most eminent intellectual leaders. Not so long ago a charter was secured for the Los Angeles University of International Affairs, to be connected with the University of Southern California. The World Federation of Educational Associations is at present also developing a plan for an international university. The International Associations of Labour have also strongly recommended the establishment of such an institution; and to catalogue the various activities in the direction of international fellowship and the encouragement of international educational and cultural coöperation, from the Rhodes Scholarships to the recent Guggenheim Foundation, would exceed the limits of this paper.

This mere mention of some of the activities conveys only an inadequate summary of what is being done to internationalise education and stimulate study between alien peoples and promote cultural contacts between students and intellectuals of the different nations. The movement is world-wide, in-

tense, earnest, prolific, diverse and intelligent. Never
ɔefore in history was there such a firm, universal purpose to bring together the peoples of all climes, supported by all the great institutions of learning, by intellectual organisations, by scholars, publicists, and
all men and women of vision, patriotism and idealism. The cultural heart of humanity the world over
is throbbing in unison with a lofty inspiration. There
seems to be general agreement among all thoughtful,
reflecting people, in every land, that the rational
method to end the barbaric madness of war and international strife is by demolishing the barriers
raised by prejudice through lack of understanding between peoples of different races and cultures, and by
enlightened contact and coöperation in cultural development establish the fact that we are all the children of One omnipotent God and can dwell together
in concord as members of one universal family.

The millennium is not yet at hand. There is a long
and perilous path yet to be traversed before we establish the Parliament of the World and the
Brotherhood of Man, but never before was the resolution so purposeful, the steps so logical, the measures so efficient as they are to-day.

The chief objection to an international university
is the fear that some one nation may be the dominat-
ing factor and seek to propagate its peculiar national
characteristics and culture. The world should not and

will not have the culture of any one people forced upon it. We are all vividly conscious of the bitter irritation which one nation aroused a few years ago when it attempted this; disastrous results followed. Perhaps the controlling factor in the unshakable, sacred union of the Allies was the deep resentment over this effort.

And so should we all feel. Each nation, every race has individuality, character, customs and culture which should be preserved and which supply important elements to our variegated civilisation, and give the joy and interest to life, *die Liebe des Lebens.* The chivalry and superb heroism, the profound philosophy, the radiant stream of literature, with its inspired poetry, unrivaled sculpture, glorious edifices, illustrious achievements in arts and letters by ancient peoples from early Babylonian days through the Chaldean, Egyptian, Indian epochs, from the days of the Incas to the Augustan Age and on to the resplendent period of the sublime Shakespeare, among all races, all peoples, nationalities and creeds, who knew neither automobile, airplane, telephone, electric light, or wireless, each within its own culture, testify to the everlasting truth that genius must be unhampered by fetters of uniformity, must be free and individual to reach the ripest, richest fruitage of spontaneous expression.

BERNARD EDELHERTZ

(Cinema: The Universal Eye)

Bernard Edelhertz, Assistant Attorney General of the United States under the Wilson administration, has been a consistent advocate of better understanding. As publisher of The American Hebrew Magazine and, until recently, chairman of the Board of Directors of the Motion Picture Theatre Owners Chamber of Commerce, New York, he devoted himself to a dissemination of good-will among people of divergent faiths and in enterprises within the film industry. In collaboration with General Will H. Hays, he was the originator of the Uniform Contract and Arbitration Boards, through which scores of perplexed motion picture exhibitors have come to adjust their differences in a spirit of fellowship. Last year, Mr. Edelhertz visited Europe, notably Russia where, in the course of an extensive personal investigation, he was in a position to foster good-will in a country that for centuries had been torn by intolerance. The results of that tour have received wide publicity and will soon appear in book form. Mr. Edelhertz is also prominently affiliated with various communal and philanthropic activities.

CINEMA: THE UNIVERSAL EYE

BY BERNARD EDELHERTZ

Fortunately for the future of mankind, our modern world is producing an increasing number of benign forces. There are, it seems to me, almost as many constructive as destructive influences—enough to safeguard the ultimate purposes of civilisation; to engender love and understanding where, in the hearts of human beings, enmity and intolerance still exist. Implements of human slaughter are being replaced by instruments that prolong life. Fratricide is giving way before the gathering impact of fraternity.

In the realm of thought, where the sturdiest minds may have succumbed—not so along ago—to the emotional frenzies of war, there is an intensified concentration on a better understanding and benevolent utilisation of Nature's secrets. Certainly, more than ordinary significance must be deduced from the fact that leading newspapers everywhere now give front page prominence to the discoveries and inventions of science, and to humanitarian endeavours in whatever field. Witness how on the morning of Professor Albert Einstein's announcement of his second great discovery, the new "field theory" overshadowed in editorial interest, politics, reparations, peace pacts and battle ships.

To me this is an event of at least three-fold import. First, it conveys unmistakable evidence that science, no matter how difficult of understanding, is achieving the front rank recognition it deserves. Second, that in the sphere of knowledge racial prejudices are unknown: Einstein, a professing Jew, receives universal acclaim. Third, that the paramount value of his new theory is sought in its potentialities to benefit all humanity rather than in its restricted mathematical implications.

And this recalls to mind the time, several years ago, when a popularisation of the relativity theory —Einstein's first momentous discovery—was attempted by certain of the more venturesome spirits in the motion picture industry. It was one branch of science seeking to pay tribute to another and, moreover, to instill in the minds of the many knowledge that only an isolatd few had theretofore enjoyed. Indeed it has been characteristic of the development of the cinema that it always sought to illuminate things for the understanding of all.

It is this agency of enlightenment that I should like to dwell on here, as it happens to be a subject with which I have become intimately familiar in the course of years. Since its very inception, even during the period of inevitable groping, it impressed me primarily as an ideal means toward better understanding among peoples of all nations and races.

Quite apart from the amusement values, which in themselves tend to bring about a clearer knowledge of the scenes and peoples portrayed, motion pictures have made tremendous strides in investing history with the vitality that hearsay and the printed page could never hope to accomplish. Out of which there is bound to emerge that good-will and human fellowship which most of us are striving for.

It is no exaggeration to say that the motion picture industry disseminates thought perhaps more impressively and effectively than any other institution. The past two decades have witnessed its rapid and consistent growth as a dominant factor in the lives of people.

Some may argue, on the basis of Professor Einstein, that the influence of the cinema is relative. But those of us who are genuinely concerned with human welfare may justly retort that a relative proportion of happiness is better than none; that, in the last analysis, we are not seeking the absolute in contentment and those other things that contribute to real happiness. And, with this in mind, the motion picture theatre does not represent merely entertainment. It spreads education and interchanges thought and happenings among different parts of the world. In this manner, films foster good-will and teach greater tolerance of other nations' problems.

Motion pictures, especially news films, are almost human, in that they have eyes that penetrate into the remotest parts of the world. They bring instantaneous expression and comprehension to people of whatever colour and creed. They speak a universal tongue and constitute the universal eye.

The motion picture machine depicts the drama of throbbing life in a manner understandable to all. Films of this informative and enlightening nature are seen by millions of people everywhere, including semi-civilised and even barbaric countries. Just visualise thousands of lenses, in every nook and corner of the globe, focussed on every worth-while occurrence, holding up the mirror to every phase of human activity the world over.

News-gathering agencies may tell us instantaneously of the outstanding events, customs and habits in this or that land. But almost invariably we receive such intelligence coloured through the eyes and reactions of the person transmitting it: On the other hand, motion pictures present the same episodes with an unfailing accuracy and realism that leave no room for doubt. And so the nations of our inhabited world are coming to regard pictures as their most dependable source of information, through which they can readily appreciate and understand and love their fellow beings, regardless of religions or nationalities.

Where the most astute statesmen may be baffled by intricate problems affecting international amity, the motion picture has the power and purpose to attain that very goal.

We of to-day are living in an age of breathtaking achievements in many fields, and most of these will be like open books to posterity largely through the recording and reproducing potentialities of the camera. Much of the immediate past is already preserved for the edification of future generations. Transoceanic flights and other aerial feats, ultra-modern warfare with all its horrors, the latest discoveries in the animal and vegetable kingdoms, astronomical wonders, geological finds of the most amazing character, the newest surgical and anatomical methods—all these, and more, have been brought within the ken of ordinary mortals through the cinema.

The Good-Will tour made by President Herbert C. Hoover just before his inauguration, was immeasurably enhanced in effectiveness by virtue of the fact that motion picture films carried every movement of that diplomatic mission to millions of people in other countries. In that way, it became an object lesson to those peoples, inspiring them to an endeavour to understand each other rather than incite them to hostility born of prejudice and misunderstanding.

America, which has accomplished in less than three hundred years a civilisation that other Continents required many centuries to build, has been singularly and fittingly responsive to the call of universal good-will. That is probably why, technically at least, motion pictures have reached a maximum of development in this country. The youthful vigour and wholesome curiosity of America is actuated by the immortal poet who sighed: "O, God, turn back the universe and give me yesterday." The thirst for knowledge and understanding here cannot be quenched by a mere allusion to musty tomes. In order that our descendants may have a clear picture of our present (their past), Americans of to-day are resolved to bequeath to them visual evidences of every momentous act, occurrence and personality. It is a wise and provident legacy which is conducive to a greater understanding of and amity for fellow humans of different colour, creed and conviction.

It is easy to imagine what untold suffering, bloodshed and hatred could have been averted in centuries past, had our forefathers had the means of to-day to see, hear and examine the causes of their enmities. Surely, the pages of history would not be so dark with the record of iniquities, political and religious strife, could the people of those days have glimpsed—as it is now possible through motion pictures, radio, telephone and kindred devices—the ulterior factors in many a human tragedy. The infuriated mujiks of Czaristic Russia might never have massacred their Jewish neighbours, had they had the means to know that the charges against the latter were trumped up; that books, and documents, which they were too illiterate to read, would have proved the Jews to be their devoted fellow citizens. Indeed, it is gladdening to know that the present rulers of Russia, despite their many imperfections, employ to a great extent motion pictures, the printed word, and other enlightening influences to make the masses harbor love instead of hatred for the Jews. And similarly every blood-stained chapter of history might now be a more cheerful tale, had there been a wide-spread existence of information at the disposal of those who were made to perpetrate deeds of violence against their fellow-men of other faiths or political hue.

But, henceforth, our leaders, rulers, friends and foes, our historic acts and our humanitarian deeds, as well as our scientific achievements, will live forever. When our grandchildren read in their books of some unusual political movement, of bitter strug-

gles, of triumphs and defeat, of principles carried
to victory and enemies of progress vanquished, they
will be able to complete the printed word by living
pictures of the actors in such human dramas. And
that will enable them to understand each other infinitely better than did their ancestors.

The celluloid pages of history will be not only
more visible but also more easily understood.

With television and other startling inventions im-
minent for utilisation, with astronomical telescopes
bringing other planets closer for observation, who
can tell but that the day is near when we shall even
behold realistic glimpses of the future.

Meanwhile, it augurs well for the theme of this
volume that the motion picture—one of the newest
yet most potent achievements of science—communi-
cates to millions of us the record of contemporaneous
human events, which cannot but stimulate better understanding among ourselves.

ABRAM SIMON

(Can Jew and Christian Understand Each Other?)

Abram Simon in his presidential message to the Central Conference of American Rabbis in 1924 suggested the "feasibility and advisibility of inviting to a conference or series of conferences religious leaders of the Church and Synagogue for a friendly discussion of those teachings and ideas that are the source or occasion of misunderstandings and prejudice, with a view to a public revelation of the findings thereof." Carrying this suggestion into effect, there was created the Joint Commission on Good-Will between Jews and Christians of the Federal Council of Churches of Christ and the Central Conference. Later Dr. Simon founded the Synagogue Council of America to establish friendly and coöperative relations within the Jewish fold. Dr. Simon is Rabbi of the Liberal Jewish congregation in Washington, where his activities have included presidency of the Board of Education and of the Columbia Hospital for Women. During the World War he was Red Cross Officer with the 79th Division, and was decorated by the German Government for humanitarian service.

CAN JEW AND CHRISTIAN UNDERSTAND EACH OTHER?

BY DR. ABRAM SIMON

J EWS and Christians are separated only by the sincerity or the insincerity of their professions of good-will. Let not the sneer of Dean Swift be true that men have just enough religion to hate, not to love one another. Jews and Christians are apart because they have made no efforts toward mutual understanding.

What keeps Christian and Jew from such a co-operation? Prejudice! A prejudice is an opinion or an emotion or a judgment made in advance of due examination. Such a judgment is usually the instinctive reaction of bias. Difference in feature and function runs through the universe of stars and seeds, of suns and souls. Infinite variety is the classic charm of infinite Nature. The soul of France does not behave like the soul of Russia. England expresses herself differently from Japan. Who asks any nation to surrender the uniqueness of her soul for the dull drab of monotonous uniformity?

Judaism claims the same privilege for the right of

its soul to independent self-revelation. Why should
the Christian Church deny this right to Judaism?
Why should Christianity claim that a New Dispensation has driven beyond the grace of God and
the favour of man the so-called Old Dispensation?
Why should any religion declare that the world is
so narrow as to have room only for one religious
message?

No matter how vigorous may be Gentile opposition to the so-called Old Dispensation, the fact remains that the Jewish religion, however inadequately appreciated, is still a thriving, spiritual enterprise. It ill becomes Christianity to enjoy the pastime of hanging crepe on the doorbells of the Synagogue. It is unbecoming a daughter of Judaism to
bespeak the premature death of her mother.

Believing that the cause which separates Jew and
Christian is not the right of our religion to exist
and to be distinctive, the conclusion is justifiable
that the source of the ill-will lies in the individuals
as Jews or as Christians, rather than in their religious
interpretations. In other words, it is not religion that
is the divisive element. It is personalities, social relationships, accumulated racial deposits with their
inevitable claims of superiority and prestige that
accentuate these differences, and separate us into
unfriendly camps. The prejudice is not against Judaism, the religion, but against Jews, as individuals

and as representing certain social and ethnic types and traits.

Of course, by all the exactions of history, the Jews ought to have been killed off the stage. Their existence is a living protest. They refuse to commit hara-kari either as an accommodation or as a penalty. Driven in upon themselves they have fought for self-preservation; and, if in the belief of their historic mission, they have cultivated the powers of resistance and persistence and qualities of mind that inspire success, they do not merit hatred or suspicion, but rather surprise and respect.

What is the cause or the occasion or the character of such prejudice?

I should divide the prejudices against the Jew in three groups. First, those resulting from the Crucifixion story in the New Testament. Second: Those resulting from the Merchant of Venice. Third: Those resulting from the anti-Semitic scholarship of racial theories, "Made in Germany."

I hesitate in writing on the Crucifixion story. I know with what spiritual tenderness and melting exaltation Christians read and ponder over this ceaseless tale of sacrifice. I wonder, however, if the Christian world will ever realise that traceable directly to this story is the age-long crucifixion of Israel.

The question which I put is this, "Why should

my children and the children of the twentieth century suffer, because of that most unhappy tragedy?"
An average Christian child can not take his eyes
from the trickling blood of nailed hands without
resting them in resentment upon the Jewish child as
Christ-killer. With the very best of intentions to the
contrary, the psychology of seeing blood creates bad
blood. No Christian child leaves the Crucifixion with
a sense of deepening affection for the Jewish child,
or even in one of pitying forgiveness of "Father,
forgive them: they know not what they do."

Can it be that Christians believe that the Jewish
people, having denied the Christ, are still under the
curse? Do they really believe that the love of
Almighty God can be chargeable with an eternal curse
on the spiritual discoverers of His Existence and
Unity?

Nor would I have Christians believe that all of
the Jews denied Jesus. The testimony of the New
Testament is that his disciples were Jews, that the
common people heard him gladly, and that his en-
trance into Jerusalem was an ovation from the multitude, singing Hosannas and waving palms. That
individual and influential priests may or may not
have liked him no more justifies the hatred for Jews
to-day than the shocking tortures of Savonarola,
Wycliffe, Huss and other martyrs should hold to
future execration of religious followers of Christian

fanaticism. Who reproached the descendants of those whose intolerance burnt witches at Salem? Nothing in recent years has been so unutterably condemned as the crucifixion of Belgium and the *Lusitania*. Yet, with whatever of horror we contemplate these crimes, no finger of rebuke is pointed at the religious beliefs of those who inspired or perpetrated these ghastly outrages.

Nor was there anything in the teachings of Jesus that could be construed as in violent contradiction to the best Jewish thought of the age. There were likely some who opposed his teaching just as to-day the restrictions of prohibition and Puritanism have violent antagonists. What certain Jewish leaders objected to at that time, and what they later on refused to accept, was the coalescence of Jesus, the man, with Christ, the Divine Atonement.

There is no doubt of it that the religion of Jesus is not the Christian religion. What did Jesus know of Original Sin, Infant Damnation, Transubstantiation, Immaculate Conception, Ascension to Heaven, the Atonement, Papal Infallibility, all the dogmas of the Apostles' or the Nicene Creed? Were Jesus to visit a modern Christian Church, his unfamiliarity with these dogmas would be most apparent. All these thoughts were as far from the mind of Jesus as the 17th or 18th Amendment from the American statesmen who wrote our Constitution.

It is, therefore, on the basis of Jesus, a Jew, in line with the highest flights of ancient prophetic teachings, lover of God and lover of his fellow-men, that Jew and Christian may find an ampler platform for mutual understanding.

We shall never be able to measure the ocean of ill-will, suspicion and mistrust for which the *Merchant of Venice* is directly responsible. If only the majestic genius of Shakespeare had not created such a misrepresentation. The constructive imagination of Shakespeare fashioned an individual, placed him in the Ghetto, dressed him in a gabardine, made him a victim of Middle Age proscription and hatred, engraved on his face and in his heart the lines and weaknesses which a cramped experience generated and called him Shylock, a son of Israel. Shylock met the level of the gallery gods of the seventeenth century.

Jews will never cease resenting this caricature of things Jewish. No matter how we may endeavour to gloss over the behaviour of Shylock, he still remains an avaricious money lender of Venice, and not typical of the Jews of Jerusalem or of the United States. Even if we attribute to Shakespeare the desire to make a universal appeal of sympathy for the Jew, the fact remains that Shylock is distasteful to our religious and social sensibilities.

Shakespeare had no other purpose than to show

the limits of a character developed under hatred and persecution. He places in glaring contrast the two noble ideals of justice and love. In order to bring both of them into striking and conflicting relief, he presents the former as embodied in the Jew, and the latter incarnated in the Christian. In order that Shylock may be an adequate representative of Justice, he must be greedy of money, bent on revenge, a hater of the Christian, and a seeker of the pound of flesh. I ask any fair-minded man if these vices are characteristic of Jews any more than they are of Christians? I ask any fair-minded man if these weaknesses are not inherent in men and women as individuals rather than the expressions of their religious loyalties? What weaknesses has Shylock in his vulgar love of money that can not be duplicated in men and women to-day of other faiths? Who has a monopoly on revenge, greed and hatred?

If Jew and Christian are to live together, they are to pull up the blinds. If Jew and Christian are to coöperate, their windows should be cleansed of all specks, smears and motes. Trying to understand one another, they may be startled at first by the glare which the blazing truth drives before their mental vision. But they will eventually grow accustomed to the new light and greet it with a cheer. They will rejoice in knowing how much they have in common either in vice or in virtue.

A third source of indiscriminate prejudice against the Jewish people comes from the double proclamation of the superior Aryan over the Semitic race, and the alleged commitment of the Jews to capitalism.

These two charges were born in the German universities. Great scholars hatched them in their fevered brains. They are the disreputable children of the Franco-Prussian war. To attempt an explanation of both of these indictments would take us far afield. My purpose is to portray and not to give a dissertation on racial and economic philosophies. Suffice it to say that the German scholars have given us a new apotheosis of race. The long-headed, fair-haired, blue-eyed race of Aryans most creatively expressed in the supremacy of the Teuton is in direct contrast to the narrow-headed, dark-skinned, curly-headed Semite who belongs by force of History and Ethnology to the Orient.

The discredited theory of the pure race has long since been the erstwhile mental pastime of scholars culminating in the tragedy of the world war, and has been magnified by the supposed relationship of the Jew to capitalism. This latest pronouncement goes down to the roots of the humblest man's understanding or misunderstanding. Nothing so inflames the labouring classes as the bluster of haughty, tyrannous and self-sufficient capitalism. It would be an easy task to balance the names of some bankers who happened to be of Jewish birth and who have long since exchanged their birthright for a mess of Teutonic pottage by the names of such outstanding leaders as La Salle, Bernstein, Karl Marx and dozens of others, haters of the capitalistic system, friends of the poor, and protagonists of the new economic revolution.

Nor would it be difficult to show how this double-barreled theory was directly responsible for the Dreyfus tragedy in France, the hundred-fold pogroms in Russia, the fiasco of the "Procotols of the Elders of Zion."

The Jew is charged with an undue worship of success, that he interprets success and power in terms of money, that the possession of money by so many bankers and brokers creates an invisible empire of Jewish finance with its dead hand upon the lever of Christian progress and civilisation; that he is not creative but reaps his inordinate rewards as distributor rather than as producer, that he is ill-bred, unscrupulous, with an eye to first advantage, lacking in self-restraint, unsensitive to the rights of others, annoyingly conspicuous and vulgarly aggressive, finding himself socially exclusive and Jewishly gregarious, and at heart swamped by materialistic longings and atheistic tendencies.

Far be it from me to exculpate the vulgarities and the flaunting insolence of individual Jews. But what

I do most strenuously resent is the indictment of all our people because of the cupidity or stupidity of some or many.

We gain nothing by alleging the same offenses in Christians. What we Jewish people ought well to cultivate is the art of self-criticism, an art whose enshrinement in the Cathedrals and Churches of Christ would be equally desirable. We Jews have our individual preferences and prejudices. And while we know what are our own objectionable traits as individuals, it becomes our first duty to clear our minds of any prejudice against the Christian either as exponent of a certain creed or as a definite social group or as an individual.

Let every Jew first sweep before his own door. His duty is to win the good-will of his fellow-man for his own inherent, individual worth. Craving for fellowship, he must have the capacity for it. The individual Jew must make himself lovable, and ask to be judged on his own merits.

There is no Jewish prejudice against the Christian. There is an amazing amount of dislike in our own ranks for those of our brethren of broken accent and foreign birth. That the Jews condemn those who left the Synagogue is no more reprehensible than the contempt which we pour on the American who betrays his country or sells his American citizenship for a foreign title. Our desire to preserve the integrity of our religion by an unwelcome ear to the music of intermarriage does not mean our objection to the melting pot of civic and political unity. We are not, therefore, a group that refuses an approach. Fraternity is an instinctive craving of our hearts.

We can best cultivate the art of mutual appreciation by dragging our souls into the open forum of public discussion and fair play. Conferences between the Jewish and Christian clergy is a desideratum. An interchange of pulpits between denominations will disclose honest differences of standpoint, and will help to clear the mind of bias and miasma.

Nothing so appeals to me as the rather recent discovery of the inscription on the Pool of Siloam. In the days of kings Ahaz and Hezekiah, engineers cut through the massive rocks to bring the nourishing waters from a great distance into the Holy City. The inscription shows how, on opposite sides, the men with pickaxes drove their incessant and well-directed blows until, through the thin partition of rock, the pickaxe of one touched the pickaxe of the other, and thus the limpid waters of life flowed in refreshing streams to the people of Jerusalem. Let us consecrate ourselves to this gigantic task. It will call for a heavy drain upon our patience, our loyalty, our courage and our sincerity. Let us together take up the pickaxe and chop away at the heap of wrongs that bar our mutual relationship. Slowly the hills will crumble;

the lies and delusions will fall to powdered dust, and from opposite sides piercing the barrier, so thin and tenuous, Jews and Christians shall beat their pickaxes into hand-grasps and their prejudices into prayers for each other's welfare.

JOHN W. HERRING

(Strange Bedfellows)

John W. Herring is an Iowan with a Mid-Western education and a penchant for nation-wide activities in the cause of religious and general education. Having received his theological training at conservative Oberlin and the Chicago Theological Seminary, he started his pastoral service at the Community Church in Chicago and then graduated rapidly to the Secretaryship of the Committee on Good-Will of the Federal Council of Churches. This brought Dr. Herring into close contact with Jews through the Joint Commission on Good-Will between Jews and Christians and led to his becoming co-chairman of the National Conference of Jews and Christians when that organisation was created in 1927. Dr. Herring is at present Field Representative of the American Association for Adult Education. His essay in this symposium indicates the thorough grasp he possesses of the subject he is treating, as a result of his numerous and intimate contacts.

STRANGE BEDFELLOWS

BY JOHN W. HERRING

THE demobilisation of racial antagonisms is a tremendously difficult task for the reason that these were forged in times of great pressure and extreme heat. They are none the less obstinate because we were quite unconscious that we were forging them. Much of that time we were consciously led by high-sounding motives; we were, however, feeding our souls upon hates that were bound to bear vile fruits in unexpected directions. No one would have dreamed, for example, that the hot tempers of the war would leave us with diseased nerves on which the Ku Klux Klan would play. Yet precisely this happened. And Americans with the psychology of the klansman are to be found everywhere, and in all ranks. "Klanism" is not membership in an organisation. It is a state of mind.

But we have gone through the worst phases of the relapse from idealism that followed the War and are at last in the frame of mind where we can begin to pick up the pieces and study our mistakes and make a new start. The first of the great mistakes that is apparent to us is that we falsely prided ourselves upon what we may call the American "neighbourhood." There have not really been any such phenomena. Judaism is a closed book to the Christian. Catholicism is a vague mystery to the Protestant. Economic and racial groups are miles apart—radio, telegraph, telephone, steam engines, automobiles and airships to the contrary notwithstanding.

May I quote on this point, excerpts from a letter written by ex-Governor Alfred E. Smith concerning the good-will movement in which the Federal Council of Churches is coöperating with representatives of Jewish agencies:

"I know of no greater need to-day than the promotion of tolerance through understanding. It has been my experience in life that the first step in the removal of prejudice is knowledge. When people of different races and traditions act together for a common cause, they soon recognise in each other not the differences that divide, but their common humanity that unites them. Just as children are taught to know by doing, so grown men and women are taught to understand by common action. Once they understand, then I have no fear of intolerance. Understanding begets sympathy and sympathy dissipates the mists of prejudice. This movement applies the fundamental principles of American Democracy, which have reared a great Nation upon the basis not of racial origin or religious creed but upon the corner-stone of the worth of the individual whatever his race or creed."

That is to say—can any agency of a group be religious? This may seem a strange question and yet there are many people who are asking it with entire seriousness. Usually we have confused the church and religion. We have assumed that the church was religion. The truth is that a church, or a synagogue, is no more religion than a college is intelligence. The point of our question depends upon what religion is.

Just to be arbitrary let us say that the religions we call Judaism and Christianity are the overwhelming desires of true Jews and Christians to be serious about the brotherhood of man and the fatherhood of God. This may be a highly unscientific or non-philosophic definition, but I am convinced that it means at least as much to my fellows of the same common garden variety as myself as if we were to speak of the cosmic urge or humanity's demand for an answer to the unanswerable.

At the expiration of an appreciable period of special interest and effort in the relationship of Jews and Christians one is forced to recognise that the three most serious barriers to human brotherliness are the

division of men into economic classes, the pigmenta-
tion of men's skins with different colours, and the
separation of men into different churches.

Protestants of course are apt to feel that the
Catholic church or the synagogue are to blame. Jews
are apt to feel that the Protestants or the Catholics
are to blame. Catholics are apt to feel that Jews or
Protestants are to blame. But, suspending the question of blame, the stark unlovely fact remains that
churches have often tended to defeat the very ideal
of brotherhood that is central in their common teaching. Some of the most glaring examples of intolerance and unbrotherliness of our day are partly
ecclesiastical in their roots.

The truth is that intolerance runs like a dark stain
through every group. As a rule the stain is darker in
majority groups. It is "safe" to be intolerant when
one has the numbers on his side. The stain is also
apt to be darker in groups of uncontrolled emotional-
ism, and of unschooled intelligence. Mob passions
find such groups defenseless prey. It is a dark commentary, too, on human sportsmanship, that the
Hindu "untouchable" or the "superior white," or
the "privileged rich," or the "Christian majority,"
or the "Briton, ruler of the sea," have a much worse
record than the weaker, or the poorer, or the smaller,
or the less civilised groups that have been their

victims. *Noblesse oblige* has never been the law of inter-group attitudes.

Thus it is no idle pleading when we urge that the chief religious duty of mankind to-day and in all days is to purge our groups of intolerance and impregnate them with an overpowering sense of the kinship of all men. Practically speaking we have been content to preach brotherhood and practise division. And we have ample evidence that the spiritual house of mankind cannot stand, never has stood, when thus divided against itself by the war between theory and practice.

It seems clearer and clearer that we have not adequately understood the nature of our problem. We have talked of brotherhood but we have never made a serious attempt to fashion a society in which brotherhood has a fair chance. To illustrate briefly: —we have so organised ourselves in water-tight groups that we are quite ignorant of one another's real selves. How many Protestants out of a thousand know anything about the inside life of a devout Catholic? And again *is not Judaism a closed book to ninety per cent. of Christianity?* Or how much does the average Jew have an opportunity to learn about the inner self of a Christian?

It is all very well to say that all we need in our society is a code of tolerance that is keyed in the philosophy of live and let live. But human nature doesn't work that way. Where ignorance is, intolerance thrives. Where understanding is, tolerance is a natural fruit. What we have done is to organise and entrench our differences. What we need to do is to organise and emphasise our agreements.

Let us not misunderstand one another. We do not plead here for the abolition of groups; for the invention of any spiritual "esperanto"; for the anemia of a life reduced to a common denominator. We plead rather for that high ideal of civilisation which can glory in variety because it has first gloried in unity. No artist can safely venture to be original until he has first mastered those indubitable truths that underlie all art. No society can afford to differentiate except as it achieves a basic unity. Let us not forget that there is a polar difference between conformity and unity: that conformity is a shallow exercise that stunts the soul, whereas unity is a supreme discovery that vitalises the soul to range onward in creative living.

Is it not obvious that our sectarianism, our denominationalism, our whole system of water-tight groups, each with its special loyalty to that which is within and prejudice against that which is without, need careful surveying and modification? If men hate or mistrust the unknown, and are kindly or at least generous towards the known, then does it not

inexorably follow that a society of mutually ignorant groups will be *a hating society*; and as a hating
society will continue to organise its klans, its wars,
its inquisitions? Is it not fair to say in the light of
1914-1918 and of our internal strife that civilisation itself hangs on our ability to build an understanding society? Does not the ultimate worth of
the League of Nations, of our mediums of common
information, of our community movements, of our
tentative steps towards religious understanding, lie
in their power to further this understanding?

We believe most firmly that we of the church have
been laggard. That the newspaper, the community
chest, the commercial association, the trade union,
have been more catholic than we. And we believe
that the church is to-day digging the gulf that may
prove its grave in its prepossession with those creedal
elements that divide mankind. But we also believe
that the average American community is surprisingly
ready for an opposite leadership from the church.

We blush to record what has taken place in the
past dozen years in scores of American communities,
where a rabbi and a minister meeting for the first
time in a community chest campaign have stumbled
onto the miracle of their common humanity and have
proceeded to a practical and deepening fellowship.
We blush because their religions divided them and
their secular activities brought them together. "Let

the secular movements in our communities do the unifying," say some. Well, why not? No,—for two reasons,—First: when the unifying of mankind is left to the community chest and the subdividing of mankind is left to the church, then the church abandons its most religious of tasks. In an exceedingly important sense it becomes less religious than the so-called "secular" community agency—And Second: there is no agency in the community with powers so uniquely suited for the task of harmonising groups to one another as the church. The church reaches the people;—and it touches them on their "caring" side. True their "care" and earnestness is often bigotry. But even bigotry is more hopeful as raw material than is the flippancy of the street.

The program of the church in the local community, if modified by this philosophy, would be moved to revolutionary things. Jews and Protestants and Catholics, modernists and fundamentalists, labour and capital, black and white, would sit down together in an infinite number of joint conferences. Age-old walls would be torn down. Loyalties would become both deeper and broader. Men would dedicate their spirits to richer and more generous living. We might hope to find the "over-soul" and to hear the universal music.

WALTER HART BLUMENTHAL

(A New Pattern of Humanity)

Walter Hart Blumenthal is a poet, critic and bibliophile, whose erudition and Weltanschauung are steeped in deep appreciation of a precious past and visions of a more ideal future. With a bent for the historical, he likes to quarry for the quaint; yet he is progressive in thought and human sympathies. His major poems are collected in "A Pageant of Moods," and "Winepress." Since 1920 Mr. Blumenthal has been associate editor of "The American Hebrew" and has participated vigorously in promulgating the idea of breaking down walls of misunderstanding and building bridges of good-will, fostered by that publication. He suggested that the endeavour toward better understanding be given permanence by the formation of a protagonist group, representing the three major religions in American life—and culminating in the organisation of such a body. Mr. Blumenthal is now Literary Editor of the "Popular Encyclopedia of the Jews," and expects to complete before long a monumental work on American Indian lore to which he has devoted more than a decade of research. He was Revision Editor of the Universal Encyclopedia in its American edition.

A NEW PATTERN OF HUMANiTY

BY WALTER HART BLUMENTHAL

THE war marked the end of an era. In its aftermath we are setting the world's house in order
—or trying to! The era of fraternisation has come.
Federation is the keynote of the times. The whole
economic basis of society compels intercourse and
interrelation. World movements are afoot. The old
battle-axe philosophies are doomed. Nietzsche is
passé.

In other words, Necessity is a strong master; and
that a growing sense of mutuality among groups of
men is a matter of compulsion, has come to be understood by the far-seeing. For the business of war is
now so titanic in its havoc that it brings even the
victors to the brink of ruin. Men are coming to
realise that if Civilisation is not to topple like a
house of cards—at least our Western Civilisation—
then we must cultivate the Will-to-Concord.

In antiquity, the life period of nations was
reckoned by the measure of their martial strength.
There was no spirit of give and take, except the give
and take of bloodshed and battle. The mediaeval

world of the Orient was completely separated and unknown to Europe of the Middle Ages; and in mediaeval Europe the Church with its ascendency would brook no rivals. Hence the spirit of concord was unknown. In the religious sphere and in the political sphere the spirit of nationalism was fostered and became paramount.

To-day in Europe, due to force and enmities, there is still a strong disinclination to lay aside national rivalries; to work in the spirit of keen coöperation.

In America alone is true effort toward better understanding prevailing, and at present in America alone is its fruition possible. This is so because not merely is the American population made up of a variety of racial strains, which necessitates coöperation if the Government is to endure as a common unit with the loyalty of all elements, but in view of the principles on which America was founded, it is necessary for the spirit of concord to take root. Aside from the variety of racial sources which constitute our population, we started out with political principles, in the experiment of 1776, which postulated as a premise that man will work together with man,—will live in harmony with his neighbour in the mutual pursuit of happiness.

The tendency of the day is towards coöperation rather than rivalry. There is coming to be a consciousness that we have passed the stage in the world's history when survival can be accomplished only through the physically fittest, through force of arms, and competition. We are coming more and more to realise that better understanding and concord are in the end more successful—even in a utilitarian sense—and more enduring than the old battleaxe philosophies.

The very nature of the making of America destined this country to be the cradle for better understanding among peoples. A study of the conditions behind the waves of immigration to America indicates that in every case the immigrants left their native lands to seek greater freedom for self-expression. They brought with them a hatred of the misunderstandings which drove them from their Old World homes, and, under the influence of American freedom and American institutions, peoples of different cultures have found that they can live together in ever-enhanced harmony. The movement for better understanding arose after the Great War. Psychologically, it could have arisen only in America. The United States had no selfish interest in the world war. After the armistice and the return of the American boys, the question naturally arose as to what it was all about. The Peace Treaty indicated that, notwithstanding America's effort as promulgated in President Wilson's idea of the League of Nations, Europe was again returning to its nationalistic concepts that would inevitably lead to the old-time hatreds and misunderstandings.

Here in America, the reaction was just the other way.

H. G. Wells, who spread the panorama of the past in his "Outline of History," well caught the spirit of the times. He probes with the penetration of a philosopher whose feet are on earth and whose head is not in the clouds. He sees on the one hand the forces of oblivion and on the other the beckoning future. "Civilisation," he says in a sentence that will not die, "is education in a race with catastrophe."

But his preoccupation with the past has not blinded him to the perils of the present or the uncertainties of an ultimate to-morrow. Though his "Outline" is bulky, there is, perhaps, more of the essence of wisdom in his slender "Discovery of the Future."

Therein, with marvellous mentality, he pleads for prevision—that mankind look forward more and backward less. Therein he states that from history may be formulated laws and lessons to guide mankind through the uncalendared future, with less of blundering and bludgeoning than marked its past. He pleads for a scientific study of futurity. For the present is but an illusion; the moment that was here like a breath is gone; the past is no more, and the only reality is the time to come. He declares that definite prognostications may be made as to the

probable course of events judged by and large, and
that national destinies may be forecast with more
than a semblance of certainty.

His word is the capstone of an edifice that had
many builders. That the trend of human events is
not fortuitous, the lives of men not haphazard and
the progress of the world not purposeless was a truth
perhaps first convincingly established by Herbert
Spencer. Darwin had restricted his findings to the
animal world including physical man. Spencer
showed that societies and civilisations undergo evolution as does palpitant life. He showed that there is
a conflict for survival in the ideas of the world of
thought as there is in the world of plants and animals. The prognosis of physical man was next carried
forward by such studies as Conklin's "Direction of
Human Evolution." But H. G. Wells, in his "Discovery of the Future," has said the first word for the
scientific control of time-to-come by the application
of laws discovered in a study of trends of the past.

This may sound rather vague, so let us be definite.
However much one may differ as to what constitutes
civilisation, there can be no doubt that concord, as
opposed to conflict, is one of its fundamentals.
Civilisation in a sense is a process of artificial regu-
lation of Nature. It harnesses waterfalls and it curbs
savage instincts. It rotates crops and it initiates birth-
control. The more primitive a people, the more com-

bative. For elemental nature knows only conflict, whereas civilisation, which is man's attempt to control and direct the forces of Nature, aims at the elimination of friction. This foresees as a finality, universal peace and good-will among men. Not inert pacifism or cloying meekness. But a sense of vigorous kinship—of fellowship in a world redeemed from profitless dissension.

The very terms "interstate commerce," "federated charities," "league to enforce peace," "society of religious liberals," "world court of arbitration," "international Red Cross," indicate the ever-widening circles of fraternisation—a growing sense of universal brotherhood, purged of cant. That, after all, rather than material advancement, measures the progress of humanity.

One must break down the fear which holds "internationalist" as a term of reproach. Cultivation of the "international mind" is a pressing need. Just as surely as primitive bands federated into tribes, tribes into city states, states into nations, so will the family of nations find concord more enlightened than conflict. As they advance from fear to freedom they will build fewer walls and more windows. The primitive mind saw in the stranger a potential enemy. That fear survives in the distrust of nation for nation, the dislike of race for race.

But mankind is shaking off the shackles of such

fears. It is coming to realise that what is different is not necessarily inferior. The new humanism—the trend toward common betterment—which the war staggered but could not slay tells us humanity is above race and that the future of the world as it spins through the firmament is the fate of humankind.

The only walls that stand between men are death, time and space. And who shall say if love, peace and work be not greater than these? Who shall say that in the new humanism that must eventually come, the Jew may not serve as seed of the new plantation; scattered throughout the world to teach man that men are one, that their likenesses are profound and their differences superficial? Who shall say if it be not the destiny of the Jew to leaven mankind into a sense of kinship? It is in the hope of that humanism that Jew and non-Jew clasp hands on the common meeting-ground of good-will and faith in the future. That is the direction in which society is inevitably tending. Let Jews justify themselves as the so-called Chosen People by choosing to be the vanguard of the new order.

Class and race consciousness lead to class and race antagonism. Race antagonism has its roots in ignorance and bigotry, and it is never judicial or scientific. It is easy to hate and despise people whom you do not know; perhaps this is a survival of an ancient instinct to repel foreigners. On the other hand, knowledge usually brings sympathy. Hope for the peace and progress of the world must rest largely upon the general cultivation of a spirit of tolerance and sympathy for other groups, classes, nations, races, than our own. The teachings of biology and of human history indicate that further social progress must lie in the direction of the *rational coöperation of all mankind.*

To this end let the Jew lend himself. He, too, must learn that social harmony and the spirit of humanity are the goals toward which mankind is tending. Contact and education will bring the death of prejudice. Contact and education are the passwords to the democratic fraternity of the future. Above all nations is humanity; above all creeds is God.

One recalls that it was Abraham Lincoln who said of his countrymen: "We shall nobly save or meanly lose the last great hope of earth." Certainly there is no greater hope for mankind than that the spirit of better understanding may prevail to save the world from the disaster that awaits the folly of further wars, racial hatreds and religious animosities.

CHANNING POLLOCK

(Barriers To Be Broken Down)

Channing Pollock, born in Washington and educated in Austria, when he was eighteen took to dramatic criticism on dailies in his native town. Then he became press representative of leading New York producers and even founded a theatre magazine which lasted for two years. Thereupon he forsook publicity on the theatre and took to playwriting for the theatre. Beginning with "A Game of Hearts" in 1900 and rising by gradations from such pieces as "Hell," the "Follies," and "The Sign on the Door," he wrote and staged such modern moralities as "The Fool," "The Enemy," and "Mr. Moneypenny." Channing Pollock believes there is room in the theatre for the play with an idea and is enamoured of the hope that even the present generation will see this belief justified.

BARRIERS TO BE BROKEN DOWN

BY CHANNING POLLOCK

WE talk—some of us—about "the prejudice against the Jew" as though it were an isolated phenomenon. As though there were no other race hatreds, and never had been any, and, therefore, this particular prejudice had to be examined, not as a symptom, but as a disease.

As a matter of fact, in some degree, pretty nearly all races hate one another, and even nations practically of the same race. The crust of friendship is so brittle that the merest incident breaks through, and immediately we are all struggling among the pieces. The English and we are much of the same blood— and there is a good deal said about blood being thicker than water. Very recently England and America were comrades in arms. And yet no one can live in England without being aware of a thinly veiled prejudice against America, and no one can live in America without frequently taking up the cudgels to combat a bitter and unreasoning prejudice against England.

Of course, this feeling is diluted by the waters of the Atlantic. If American and Englishman lived together in the same city—in the same street—it would be many times as strong. The Jew who feels himself an unique victim of discourtesy should consider the position of the English actor in the Lambs' Club!

Where different races are compelled to consort together the results usually are of a nature to make friction between Jew and Christian seem, in comparison, the running of well-oiled machinery. I remember a year in Prague, when Prague was in Austria, and divided almost equally between Czechs and Germans. Each race had its own language, of course, and its own shops and schools and theatres. I remember being mobbed one day because I spoke German to a sausage vendor in the Czechish Quarter!

The Jew in this country is foolishly but explainably sensitive to ridicule, and feels himself injured by cheap jokes at his expense on the variety stage and in the comic weeklies. And yet, from the beginning of my recollection, an absurd and offensive caricature has been the accepted type of the Englishman. And of the Irishman. And the Frenchman. We speak contemptuously of the race that produced Dante and Michelangelo as "wops."

Race prejudice, of course, is atavistic, and, in its

modern manifestations, the result of ignorance and of malicious misrepresentation. Men are without that prejudice in direct proportion to their culture and enlightenment. The dull and uneducated always judge by a composite, forming that composite from the dregs at the bottom—from the material they know.

To the man who does not know, and has no opportunity of knowing, Stephen Wise, or Daniel Frohman, or Otto Kahn, or Nathan Straus, or Abraham Flexner, the Jew is an unclean and illiterate person who shuffles along a pavement. This man forgets that there are as many unclean and illiterate Christians who shuffle along pavements. He hears a great deal more of the better kind of Christian—of George Washington and Abraham Lincoln—than of the better kind of Jew. The man in the street knows that Roosevelt was more or less of his own blood; he doesn't know Disraeli was a Jew.

Of course, as I have said before, intolerance is not confined to one race—no more than any other vice or virtue. Fundamentally, I wrote *The Fool* to lift my feeble voice in a cry for brotherhood, to lift my hand against the absurd and artificial barriers of creed and dogma. The thing that has made me happiest about the astounding success of the play is that it has reached peoples of all races and all religions.

In *The Fool* I identified the Christ—and I am

using "the Christ" to mean "the King," and "the King" to mean THE GOOD, because I don't know whether what spoke to Daniel Gilchrist was Christ, or the man to whom he gave his coat, or his own better self; being sure only that, in so far as that voice helped him in his hour of need, it was a Divine Voice—I identified the Christ by having him say: "I am a Jew." I did that to remind my auditors that the first Christian was a Jew. And yet, when I spoke in a fashionable synagogue, and talked of Moses, and Confucius, and Buddha, and Mohammed, and Jesus, I was followed by a rabbi who said resentfully that his congregation was not accustomed to the mention of Christ on Purim Night . . . of that Christ who was one of the outstanding teachers of brotherhood and of brotherly love!

This, of course, is ignorance and egotism of the same type we have been decrying in the Christians. . . . In THE AMERICAN HEBREW I find an heroic anecdote of a little girl who, hearing of the Cru-cifixion, ran home crying: "My father is a Jew, and he never killed anybody." First, that brings us back to the old falsehood that the Jews crucified Christ. And, second, what if they had? Would they have been the only people who ever executed a prisoner who should not have been executed? And, if some-one told how America hanged John Brown, should you think me heroic, or only idiotic, if I ran home crying: "My father is an American, and he never killed anybody"?

A good deal of most persecution is in the minds of the persecuted. The Jew imagines some of the prejudice against him in America, and makes too much of that ninety per cent. of the rest which arises from common ignorance. He begins to carry a chip on his shoulder. He must not stand aloof in bitter superiority, sensitive to silly hatred and quick to hate in return. He must not deny the faults and the objectionable traits that are his—as there are faults and objectionable traits in every race and in every individual. He must try to correct them, not to bristle at their mention.

All races that have had the worst of it are sensitive. But perhaps one reason for the present rub is that the Jew is too self-conscious—*too* sensitive. There are twenty-eight Christians in *The Fool*, and most of them are pretty unpleasant Christians. I have had no protest from the Christians, but when, in the printed play, I described one of the dishonest labour agitators as "faintly Semitic" I had dozens of letters from all over America. One very rich Christian in the play says, "Whoever heard of a poor Jew?" More letters. The fundamental rule of the dramatist, to make his characters talk as they would talk in real life, must be suspended when that talk might include a slighting allusion to the Jew. These letters, of course, like the prejudice against the Jew, come from the ignorant. It remained for a very wise and great Jew to observe: "How can we be insulted by the suggestion that our race is so thrifty, and industrious, and full of care for its own, that other races never heard of 'a poor Jew'?"

The results of prejudice against the Jew in America are almost negligible. Governmental injustices, of course, are few, and becoming fewer. Business discrimination is little, growing less, and is more than equalized by the advantage given the Jew by his vision, his imagination, his industry, and his business ability. In the arts there are no prejudices and all men are equal. Socially, the Jew suffers—largely from his own fancies, partly from his giving importance to the behaviour of the ignorant and the ill-bred, in a degree from genuine discourtesy and boorishness springing from a prejudice of which he is the victim here very little more than the American in England or the Frenchman in America.

The Jew is merely a curved inch in a vicious circle. So long as prejudice endures he cannot hope to be wholly exempt from it. And prejudice will endure, in an ever-diminishing degree, until education and understanding penetrate the crust of inherited tendencies and the dust of ages. Until, as I said in *The Fool*, the Christians really believe in Christ and the Jews really follow Moses.

PART III

THE PROBERS PRESENT THE
HISTORICAL BACKGROUND

CHARLES P. FAGNANI

(Joshua Ben Joseph of Nazareth)

Charles Prospero Fagnani is a theologian of the modernist school who has contributed to the spiritual enlightenment of many clergymen sent into pulpits by the Harvard Divinity School and the Union Theological Seminary. Born and educated in New York City, he started his career as a teacher in the public schools, but finally turned to theology and was ordained in the Presbyterian ministry. He served several congregations in and about the metropolis to gain practical experience before he presumed to teach. With a preparatory training as teacher in theology gained during nearly twenty-five years in the Harvard Divinity School, he came as professor of Old Testament language and literature to Union Theological Seminary, his alma mater, in 1915. He was made professor emeritus in 1926, and now resides in Paris. His most critical contribution to Old Testament study is a volume entitled "The Beginnings of History According to the Jews."

JOSHUA BEN JOSEPH OF NAZARETH

BY CHARLES P. FAGNANI

IS it not time wasted to discuss the thorny subject of religion under any of its aspects, unless there be a preliminary agreement that all prejudice, heat and evil speaking be rigidly excluded and the discussion be conducted on a purely impersonal and intellectual plane?

If this course is agreed upon nothing can be more profitable than a mutual interchange of views for the sake, not of bringing about agreement, which is unnecessary, but understanding and clarity which are most desirable.

We all of us are, and always will be, seekers for more truth and it is as ill becoming as it is futile for any individual or any group to set up as an ultimate authority on debatable matters. Yet it is this very assumption of knowing the whole truth which is the characteristic mark of all religious bodies.

The religions of the world, with a single, solitary exception, may all be properly classified under one category, namely, as Religions of Worship. By worship is meant the various rites, ceremonies and observances which have the Divinity for their object. All these religions stress worship and the manner of worship as being of supreme concern to their God or Gods, so much so that fellowship is refused to those who will not conform. The worship, in fact, constitutes the religion—and religiousness is tested by correctness in, and zeal for, worship.

This ritual is based on doctrine or teaching that professes to reveal the nature, character and requirements of the God and the manifestations he has made of himself in the past, a past usually far distant. The doctrines are to be found in a sacred book to which is assigned infallible trustworthiness and divine authority. Acceptance of the doctrine is necessarily involved in adherence to the ritual of worship.

There is one, and only one, religion that is different from all the others, and that one is to be seen in the teaching of the great prophets of Israel whose line culminated in the last and greatest of them, Joshua ben Joseph of Nazareth, better known under the Greek form of his name as Jesus.

This "prophetic" religion, as we may call it for convenience, has the unique characteristic that it presents God as not being concerned or interested in worship offered to himself—in rites and ceremonies, the distinctively "religious" activities, as usually understood; but as putting supreme insistence on the practice of justice, righteousness and friendliness among men.

We would naturally expect that such a religion, a religion that treats worship as negligible or, at most, optional, would be looked upon with the utmost disfavor by the priestly classes whose interests and emoluments have to do with worship.

We would likewise expect that the state or the government would be suspicious of a doctrine that made justice and equity the things God cares for most.

And so we are not surprised when we see Amos assailed by the Priest at Bethel, Jesus on Golgotha condemned by Church and State, and Stephen stoned to death for speaking against the Temple.

The essential teaching of "prophetic" religion may be summed up as stressing the Fatherhood of God, the Brotherhood of Man, and the establishment on earth of the "Kingdom of God," or the organisation of the real democracy, which involves world-wide coöperation for the common good.

We must now consider the question whether it is Judaism or Christianity that comes nearer to presenting to the world this Prophetic Religion.

Both of these terms, Judaism and Christianity, need to be carefully defined and delimited before we can get even a tentative answer to this question. For both names are too broad and too vague to be of immediate use and this because each is the result of compromise.

Judaism was born of the coming together of Canaanism and Prophetism; Christianity, of the merger of Prophetism with Hellenism.

In Reform Judaism we witness a movement whose unconscious genius is the purification from its admixture of Canaanism.

In the nascent movement in the Protestant churches called Modernism, we have perhaps a similar instinctive attempt to separate the Prophetism of Jesus from the Hellenism of Paul.

It is a fact that must more and more attain to general recognition that historical Christianity goes back to Paul as its founder and not to Jesus.

Jesus lived and died a loyal Jew. He was not a Christian.

Jesus was not a Trinitarian, Jesus did not proclaim himself God, he did not claim worship, he had no idea of founding a new religion which should displace the religion of the prophets.

For 2,000 years the Jews have been martyred because of their rejection not of Jesus but of "Christ."

In spite of unspeakable suffering they have steadfastly refused to· believe that the prophet of Nazareth was the Saviour-God of Paul, of Hellenism, and of historic Christianity.

Protestantism committed a fatal blunder when,

after throwing off the yoke of the Papacy, it substituted for it the more disastrous tyranny of an "inspired" Book.

It is part of the general confusion that besets the whole subject, that in dividing the printed Bible into Old and New Testaments or Covenants, the division was not made in what could be claimed to be the right place.

This would be not between Malachi and Matthew, on the basis largely of the difference in the original languages, but between Luke and John.

For the first three Gospels, the so-called *synoptists*, save for some later Christian elements, can be plausibly considered as Jewish documents and as belonging to the Jewish religion. It is not until we come to the fourth gospel that we find ourselves unmistakably in the atmosphere of Paulinism and Hellenistic Christianity.

Is it not an infinite pity that the synagogue, in giving up and disowning the sublime prophet that belonged to her, should thereby have ignorantly connived at the appropriation and monopolisation of him which was made by the Christian Church?

But the synagogue knew not what she was doing, and may not the time come when she will assert her indisputable claim to the Jesus of the Synoptic Gospels, leaving to the Church the Christ of Paul and of John?

Nay, the time seems already to have come, for do we not read in the words of Rabbi Stephen S. Wise, "Jesus was not a being come down from heaven, but one who *attained* to heavenly heights. He was not a God who walked on earth like a man but a human who walked with God on earth. He was not a God who lived humanly but a man who lived divinely. He was not a being who died that others might live but a man who so lived that men need not perish. Let it never be forgotten that he was ours and we might have been his, as in truth and spirit we are his. To us he belongs—not his Church, but he—the man, the Jew, the prophet."

So it is that when the Ghetto Jew execrates the name of Jesus, it is not Jesus that he thus ignorantly condemns but the Pauline Christ on whose account he has borne the badge of shame and contempt all down the ages.

When the Reform Jew honours Jesus in the company of Amos, Hosea, Micah, Isaiah, Jeremiah, as the supreme exponent of Israel's Prophetism, it is not because he has leanings towards Trinitarianism, nor is it with a view to becoming a candidate for baptism. The Jew believes in the religion *of* Jesus, he cannot bring himself to accept the religion *about* Jesus.

The religion about Jesus is historic Christianity.

"Through the beliefs associated with the incarnation, crucifixion and resurrection of Christ," as one has said, "the world became divided into a congregation of the saved and a congregation of the damned:

"The Old Covenant was superseded by the New;

"The Chosen People became the Rejected People;

"Outlaws and outcasts with the brand of Cain, the villains of the drama of Salvation;

"Enemies of God and of mankind."

Thus the Jews began the weary pilgrimage in their *Via Dolorosa* which has continued to this day.

The religion of Jesus is the religion of the Prophets that stresses the Oneness and Fatherhood of God and the Brotherhood of man.

Is the religion of Jesus enough?

Judaism says, Yes. Christianity says, No.

What would Jesus himself say?

Christianity centers on the doctrine of salvation from hell through the substitutionary sacrifice of Christ, who died to satisfy the Justice of God, thus enabling him to pardon men for the sin inherited from Adam.

This, in substance, is the scheme worked out by Paul starting with the belief common to his time, that the second and third Chapters of Genesis give us actual history.

In the religion of Jesus, God is a just and tender

Father, who forgives a prodigal son when he comes back, simply because he loves.him and not because an innocent victim has suffered in his stead.

It is the Pauline belief in the Fall of Adam that makes necessary an atonement through Christ. But if Adam is not historical and the Fall is not historical, then the Atonement is not necessary and the religion of Jesus stands forth freed from all the additions and complications that the theological speculations of the early Church have added to it.

Paul's elaborate system of theology is not found in the first three gospels.

Is it possible that the movement called Modernism may turn out to be a new and greater Reformation in which there will be a development away from the philosophical elaborations of the Pauline theology, back to the simple religion of Jesus with its two sublime assumptions, the Love of God and the Worth of Man?

Who knows?

Is it possible that Judaism will tend more and more to minimise its belief in the divine obligation of its ritual and its age-long practises, and will put its main emphasis on the pure religion of the greatest of the prophets—the Jewish Jesus of the Synoptists?

Who can tell?

HENDRIK WILLEM VAN LOON

(GREAT IS DIANA)

Hendrik Willem Van Loon has been recently appraising "Man the Miracle Maker" This, his latest book, which traces the fascinating story of inventions, is in line with his previous studies of mankind. His first was "Ancient Man," followed by "The Story of Mankind," then "The Story of the Bible," and next the story of man's attempt to break the chains of intolerance which bound him to the earth, in the much disputed book, "Tolerance." Mr. Van Loon's searchings have probed history, art and literature. These permeated his writings whether as a correspondent watching the Russian Revolution, or reporting Germany's work in Belgium during the war, or as a lecturer on history at Cornell. The Van Loon style has been imitated by many. The present essay is an excellent example both of Mr. Van Loon's literary method and his mode of thought.

GREAT IS DIANA

BY HENDRIK WILLEM VAN LOON

I MUST have been five years old when I heard
the story for the first time. My opinion of the
Ephesians thereafter was very low indeed. To meet
a perfectly nice and gentle soul like Paul with halle-
lujahs for a wicked pagan goddess was not at all
what one might have expected of a highly civilised
community like Ephesus. I was quite sure that if
Paul would only come to Rotterdam, we would give
him a very different reception.

Fortunately for Paul and unfortunately for us, he
never came. The Shah of Persia came and we had a
wonderful time throwing bricks at this gilded
Majesty.

And now, after forty years, I have come to the
conclusion that the poor Ephesians were not really
such very bad people and hardly deserved the rep-
utation for short-sighted selfishness which later generations bestowed upon them.

Of course, if they had been hard-headed and practical men of business, their Goldsmiths' Local No.

47 would have called together a meeting and after a long debate they would have appointed a committee to investigate the possibilities of the crucifix trade. If this committee had reported a possible future in the new article of commerce, they would have then dropped Diana for the benefit of the new divinity.

But I doubt whether even such a committee as suggested above would have declared in favour of a too abrupt change of policy. It takes entirely different dies and moulds and forms and a different technique to turn out Dianas and crucifixes. It would have meant millions of drachmas in new machinery. No, the Ephesians were right when they refused to risk their sound old investments for a new enterprise which looked exceedingly uncertain (to say the least) ; and as for their turbulent local enthusiasm, what else could we people of the twentieth century have expected of loyal citizens who were supposed to boost the interests of their home-town at all costs? Indeed, it seems to me that these last ten years I have heard nothing but the same ancient yell, rendered in at least two-score languages.

"Great is Diana of the Ephesians!"
Correct.

But how about the virtues of the French? They are equally great. And so we chant, "Great are the virtues of the Gallic race!"

And how about the British? They are, if anything, even greater. Let us intone, "Great is the incomparable superiority of the English people!"

How about the Teuton? A hundred thousand professors, doctors, Privatdozenten solemnly render the national anthem of Yale University and add, "Great are the Dianas of Berlin!"

And so it goes and so it went and so it shall continue to go, world without end and Dianas without comparison, Amen.

I have never heard a sermon upon the subject. In the first place I gave up the habit of listening to sermons long ago, and in the second place, if it were used as text for a little homily, I am certain that the poor Ephesians, as bad guessers of future commercial possibilities, would have been denounced with bitter sarcasm and that would have filled my heart with sorrow.

For as the world is run nowadays, we have got to be on the side of our own Diana, or suffer the consequences.

A certain admiral (it was an admiral, wasn't it?) under the stress of a great emotion, once uttered a platitude which afterwards in the hands of unscrupulous people became a sort of *Lebensphilosophie* of the very worst sort. He drank a toast to his country and added the ominous words, "May it ever be right, but, right or wrong, my country!"

Our modern world is based upon that very sentiment which was first of all heard in the streets of
Asia Minor. Our own little gods are very great and
by implication all other little gods (and big ones,
too) are very small and should not be tolerated
within the limits of our own backyard, except as
occasional visitors.

This, however, is an era of specialisation.

Such wholesale shouting of a mob of hungry sou-
venir peddlers as was done in Ephesus is entirely out
of style in an age which provides us with special
pipes and razors for the different days of the week
and with glasses for every social occasion from rob-
bery to quite formal tea with the Archbishop of Can-
terbury.

The Ephesians knew this and they have reorgan-
ised along entirely new lines which assure them a
maximum of success with a minimum of effort. National Ephesianism was comparatively easy. Patriotism and gin were ever closely related and in Europe
at least it is still quite easy to gather a mob of enthusiastic hoodlums for the purpose of howling down
even the most intrepid of enemies.

In America the problem is a little more complicated, for synthetic rum is a very unreliable substance and the staunch citizen who is under its influence may suddenly turn against the hand that has
just fed him and, having been hired to shout

"Hooray for Coffee with Milk," he may whoop it up for "Milk with Coffee," which, as all connoisseurs of the noble bean know, is an entirely different article of consumption.

Hence in America the matter is given that careful attention which correspondence schools of embalming and classical dancing call "individual instruction." And almost every person or group of persons is now provided with a few Ephesians of his or their own. They are not exactly Patron Saints, but they are just as faithful in their attendance to duty. Day and night they guard their victim or victims. And they will go to almost any limit to uphold the greatness of their own Diana as opposed to that of their neighbour's Minerva.

Do you want a few names? There is Brother Sumner, with his close comrade, the Justice, who have appointed themselves Ephesians-in-extraordinary to all the writers of our land. There is good old Henry of Detroit, who never had a lesson in his life and is proud of it. A genius absolutely without an equal along his own line. And the very opposite in every other line. Above all, a faithful Ephesian when he detects the slightest spark of Sinaic lightning.

There is that excellent divine in New York (I have forgotten his name just now) who is the pet Ephesian of all scientists and who will shout his "Great is the Jahweh of Genesis" right in the middle of the meeting of the American Society of Anthropologists.

I need not go on with my list. It is enough that I have shown you how to recognise the species. The intelligent reader can do the rest.

At the end of the lectures which in days gone by I used to give, there always was some sweet motherly woman in the gallery who asked me in the midst of my despondent wails whether I could not see a rosy lining to my clouds of doubt, and whether I could not send my audience home with a word of hope.

That was easy. One could always hope that they would go home to a good dinner.

But this time I feel myself utterly stumped. I have no message of hope.

The Ephesians are as old as the hills. They are bad in the East and they are equally bad in the West, they are terrible in New York and they are worse in Moscow. This cannot be avoided, as they are recruited from among the honest dumb-bells of every civilisation. The dumb-bells outnumber the others at the ratio of——to——. As soon as this ratio shall have been changed in favor of those whose brain is something more than a receptacle of four-letter words, the Ephesians shall die of emotional under-nourishment.

Judging by present conditions, that makes them ideal candidates for life insurance.

WILLIAM H. P. FAUNCE

(Ahead of His Time)

William H. P. Faunce has been president of Brown University since 1899. Deriving from an old Massachusetts family, Dr. Faunce entered the ministry in 1884 and was, preceding his call to Brown, pastor of the Fifth Avenue Baptist Church in New York. President Faunce has been in constant contact with many universities and colleges in America and abroad, serving as lecturer in higher institutions of learning in Great Britain and in Germany. His deepest concern, next to the youth in his charge, is in movements for international understanding and coöperation. He is president of the World Peace Foundation and Director of the Institute of Social and Religious Research. Dr. Faunce has published several books, particularly "The New Horizon of State and Church," and "Facing Life," which deals with the puzzled college undergraduate in search of a way out of the fog and confusion of post-adolescence. Dr. Faunce is chairman of the Permanent Commission on Better Understanding.

AHEAD OF HIS TIME

BY WILLIAM H. P. FAUNCE

ON the shore of the Seekonk River in the City of Providence stands a modest monument to the man who founded Rhode Island and enunciated the great principle which lies at the foundation of the United States Government. In 1635 he was "enlarged" out of Massachusetts. In 1636, after wandering through the forests for six weeks with a few loyal companions, he landed from his frail canoe and was greeted by friendly Indians with the famous salutation: "What cheer, Netop?"

No wonder Massachusetts was glad to have him depart, for he was a century ahead of his time—far in advance of most civilised states to-day. The Massachusetts autocracy could not deny his noble character, his spotless rectitude. But they said he had "windmills in his head." Indeed he carried under that broad hat an idea that was esteemed revolutionary by all known governments.

To put it bluntly, and in his own words, the

earth-shaking idea was this: "It is the will and command of God that . . . permission of the most paganish, Jewish, Turkish, or anti-Christian consciences and worships be granted to all men in all nations and countries."

Here was a solitary pioneer, daring to face not only Massachusetts, but Great Britain and all Europe, and to advocate the complete separation of church and state! Here was a Christian clergyman pleading for the freedom of Jews and anti-Christains! Here was a graduate of Cambridge University, brought up in the established church of England, pleading that no form of religious belief should ever be supported by any state, affirming that religion is an experience of the individual soul in contact with God, and that no man's conscience can be forced by any court or any government under heaven!

No wonder he was "enlarged," or, as we should say, expelled. For a thousand years the doctrine of the necessary union of church and state had entrenched itself in European history. Freedom of conscience for the individual was not asserted by Luther or any leader in the Reformation. *"Cujus regio, ejus religio"*—"the religion of the country is the religion of each man in it"—was the decision of a famous church council. If religion was essential to the welfare of the people, then the state surely could not neglect it. In the very year that Williams arrived

in Massachusetts the General Court passed this resolution: "It is ordered that henceforth no man shall
be admitted to the freedom of this commonwealth
but such as are members of the churches within the
limits of this jurisdiction." No voters except church
members, and no church members except on approval
of the clergy—such was the compact and militant
theory on which Massachusetts based its future.
Thank heaven for one young prophet of religion
who could not accept it, who faced banishment and
death sooner than surrender "soul-liberty" to a
powerful hierarchy.

In 1764 Brown University was founded near the
spot where Roger Williams landed, and his principle
of soul-liberty was written into its charter. Two provisions in that document are of immortal significance.
The first is this: "The public teaching shall in general respect the sciences." Yet in the year 1929
scores of colleges in the United States dread the sciences, and admit teachers of science only after a theological inquisition. The second unique provision of
the charter is this: "Into this liberal and catholic institution"—many good men to-day are afraid of the
word "liberal" and still more afraid of "catholic"—
"shall never be admitted any religious tests, but on
the contrary all the members thereof shall forever
enjoy full, free, absolute and uninterrupted liberty
of conscience." Those sonorous adjectives, so un-

usual in a legal document, reveal the depth of emotion which lay behind the action of the founders.

At that time all the colleges and universities of Europe would have declined to make such a declaration. Would it not seem to imply disparagement of all religious faith? Would it not open the doors to atheism, to anarchy, to subversion of all established government? Such a declaration made by the leaders of the French Revolution would be quite natural. But in Rhode Island it was made by a Corporation consisting wholly of members of Christian churches —22 Baptists, 5 Episcopalians, 5 Quakers and 4 Congregationalists. It remains to-day unaltered and inviolable, and its spirit is reflected not only in the whole history of Rhode Island but in the Constitution of the United States of America.

Are we true to the great principle of Roger Williams to-day? I wish that every American citizen might read the excellent biography of Williams written by the late Oscar Straus. But to read is not enough. We must adopt as our own, in every church and synagogue, in every town and city and state, in every act of the Federal Government the fearless and far-reaching faith of Roger Williams.

We may well ask every man who aspires to either religious or political leadership in America whether he accepts the principles of Roger Williams, now incorporated into the belief of the free churches and made a part of the Constitution of the United States. It does not mean religious neutrality. It does not mean mere secularism, and indifference to spiritual values. It means that those values are too high and sacred to be affirmed, or defined, or expounded by the secular arm. It means that a man's attitude toward his God is beyond the reach of any legal code or any judicial body and that religion, where free, is likely to prevail.

When any man is nominated for high political office, we have no right to impose any ecclesiastical or theological test. His religion concerns his own conscience. He may belong to any religious body that exists, or to none at all. But we have a right to ask whether he fully accepts the American principles of the entire and perpetual separation of civil and ecclesiastical authority.

Never while America stands shall any legislature or congress impose any restrictions on the creed of any citizen. And never while America stands shall any church lay hands on any government officer or any legislative body and attempt to control governmental action in order to maintain any religious creed. This was the faith of the solitary Roger Williams. It is now the principle cherished by 120,000,-000 Americans.

But the bare affirmation of a principle is not enough. It must be translated into action, must be interwoven with all the daily life of our citizens. If we believe with Roger Wiliams, we shall never vote for or against any candidate for political office on religious grounds alone. We shall do our best to minimise sectarian and racial barriers. We shall judge every citizen by his character and ability rather than by his theological creed. We shall in social life steadily try to see through the other man's eyes and catch his point of view. We shall often remind the Christian that Christ and all His apostles were loyal Jews and never deserted their ancestral faith. We shall constantly remind the Jews that the most influential Jew in history is the Man of Galilee. We shall build an America in which Jew and Christian, Protestant and Catholic, shall worship the God of Washington and Lincoln and perpetuate the Government they established or saved.

FRANCIS P. DUFFY

(RELIGIOUS FREEDOM IN AMERICA)

Francis P. Duffy is a native of Canada, a product of the parochial and high school system and of St. Michael's College, Toronto University, where he served as a pupil teacher. Followed years of study and tuition in the United States and his ordination to the priesthood in 1896. For fourteen years he was professor of logic and metaphysics at St. Joseph's Seminary at Dunwoodie, N. Y., and was sometime editor of the New York Review Journal of Philosophy and Theology. But Father Duffy came into public prominence when he went to the Mexican border as chaplain of the 69th, New York, and then overseas with the Rainbow Division in October, 1917. He emerged from the War as probably the most famous of the chaplains, with distinguished service honours from the British and French governments and his adopted United States. Since 1921 Father Duffy has been rector of Holy Cross Church in New York City. He is a member of the Permanent Commission on Better Understanding.

RELIGIOUS FREEDOM IN AMERICA

BY FRANCIS P. DUFFY

THERE is no room for religious intolerance in America. The very nature of our institutions forbids it. The diverse character of our population should cause its perpetual banishment from our midst. Bigotry should find no place in a land founded on the principle of equal rights for all and special privileges to none. It should find no opportunity to make its presence felt in a government that guarantees civil liberty and religious freedom to all who come within its jurisdiction. Every religious group is entitled to the same consideration, the same civil and political equality so long as its tenets and practices do not conflict with the standards of morality as prescribed by the law of the land.

Unfortunately traces still remain of the old order when fanaticism and bigotry prevailed. In our American life we have established toleration of all religious groups, permitting them all to worship

God according to their several lights. This is an established fact. But even to-day we discern outcroppings of the old fanaticism, manifestations of an ancient order. While there is no restrictive legislation, Catholics are discriminated against in the matter of franchise and election to civil service. Catholics, no less than the Jews, in certain parts of the United States, are still being made the target of abuse and calumny. Vile accusations are levelled against them. The Catholics are accused, as formerly, of conspiring for political power and other acts inimical to the State. But such accusations fall to the ground when the truth is known.

Catholics were among the signers of both the Declaration of Independence and the Federal Constitution. During the formative period of the American government (the administrations of Washington and Adams), the Irish Catholics took an important part against over-centralisation of governmental power. But they never organised as a political party or anything of the sort. Such pronouncements as they made corporatively concerning American liberty and its institutions were authoritative only when included in what are known as the Pastoral Letters of the American Hierarchy. These letters were a reply to the vile and bigoted attacks upon the church, and those of 1837 a condemnation of the outrage committed in the burning of an

Ursuline convent in Charlestown. What we read in these letters reflects in a measure the attitude of the Catholic Church and its followers in our country to-day. A few excerpts from these letters should prove illuminating.

In the Pastoral Letter of 1837, issued by the Third Provincial Council of Baltimore, runs the following statement: "We (Catholics) owe no religious allegiance to any State in this Union, nor to its general government. No one of them claims any supremacy or dominion over us in our spiritual or ecclesiastical concerns; nor does it claim any such right or power over any of our fellow-citizens, of whatsover religion they may be; and if such a claim was made, neither would our fellow-citizens nor would we submit thereto."

No less eloquent in expression but more direct in statement is the Catholic pronouncement for religious liberty as found in the Pastoral letter of 1884, issued by the Third Plenary Council of Baltimore. A portion of it reads as follows: "We think we can claim to be acquainted with the laws, institutions and spirit of the Catholic Church, and with the laws, institutions and spirit of our country; and we emphatically declare that there is no antagonism between them. A Catholic finds himself at home in the United States; for the influence of his Church has constantly been exercised in behalf of individual rights and popular liberties. . . . We believe that our country's heroes were the instruments of the God of Nations in establishing this home of freedom; to both the Almighty and to His instruments in the work we look with grateful reverence; and to maintain the inheritance of freedom which they have left us, should it ever—which God forbid—be imperilled, our Catholic citizens will be found to stand forward, as one man, ready to pledge anew their lives, their fortunes, and their sacred honour."

The fight for religious liberty in America is of long duration and began with the dawn of the colonial period in our nation's history. The early settlers knew what it meant to be denied the right of freely worshipping God in their own way; for most of them had come to this land in order to escape religious persecution abroad. But many of them believed in freedom of worship only in so far as it pertained to themselves. Once established in the enjoyment of this freedom, they denied it to others who happened to differ with them in their mode of worship.

From the pages of colonial history there emerges the picturesque figure of Thomas Dongan, Irish Catholic and soldier of fortune, who stood forth as one of the greatest champions of civic and religious liberty ever sent over by England to govern our colonial possessions. After his appointment to the governorship of the province of New York in 1682,

he convened the first representative assembly at Fort
James within the present city limits on Oct. 14,
1683. Under the wise supervision of Dongan, this
assembly passed an act called "A Charter of Liberties," in which, among other provisions, the right of
religious liberty was solemnly proclaimed. Dongan's
principles of government passed into the framework
of our Constitution and greatly influenced the Magna
Charta of our Constitutional liberties.

Students of history will recall the noble service in
behalf of religious liberty rendered by such champions as Roger Williams and James Oglethorpe. But
they will also recall that a Catholic nobleman was
the first to proclaim the principle of religious freedom in America and to carry it into practice through
the Toleration Act which was passed in Baltimore in
1649.

According to George Petrie's "Church and State
in Early Maryland," we note the following instructions, to begin with, given out by Lord Baltimore to
the first settlers: "His Lordshippe requires his said
governor and Commissioners that in the voyage to
Maryland they be very carefull to preserve unity and
peace amongst all the passengers on Shippboard, and
that they suffer no scandall nor offense to be given
to any of the Protestants, whereby any just com-
plaint may hereafter be made, by them in Virginia
or in England, and that, for that end, they cause all

acts of Romane Catholique Religion to be silent upon all occasions of discourse concerning matters of Religion."

In Lord Baltimore's instructions to the governors of the colony from 1636 to 1649 there is included an oath which had to be administered or taken by each one of them. According to this oath, a governor had to swear that he would refrain from troubling, molesting or discountenancing any person professing the Christian faith; and "that he would make no difference of person, in conferring offices, favours, or rewards, for or in respect of religion, but merely as they should be found faithful and well-deserving, and endued (endowed) with moral virtues and abilities." It also provided that "he (the governor) would protect the person molested and punish the offender."

To understand how the Toleration Act of 1649 came into being, it must be borne in mind that, after 1643, non-conformists, driven out of Virginia because of their refusal to accept the Established Church, had settled in Maryland in large numbers. The Act itself was passed by an assembly the majority of whom were Catholics. It is believed that this Act, which rather curiously specifies belief in the Trinity, was not all that Lord Baltimore himself desired. It should also be noted that the death of Leonard Calvert, Lord Baltimore's brother, who had guided most of the affairs of the colony, deprived it of valuable personal leadership after 1647. Moreover, the Act makes no reference to the Jewish people, although all historians are agreed that Lord Baltimore's toleration of them was manifest on many occasions.

If Lord Baltimore failed to mention the Jews in the Toleration Act, one can readily guess the reason why. At that early period the Jewish people were so few and far between among the settlers that they were simply ignored or lost sight of. It may prove of interest in this connection to point to the historical fact that at the time when the Toleration Act was passed, in 1649, there were no Jews in England. They had been expelled from England in 1290. Manasseh ben Israel's agitation for their return did not come to Cromwell's attention until 1655. It would appear, therefore, that Jews did not enter into the consciousness of Lord Baltimore or anyone else to whom religious tolerance had any meaning.

The gist of the Toleration Act is contained in the manifesto that no person professing the Christian faith, who was a resident of the colony, should be made to suffer for, or in respect to, his or her religion.

That this liberty applied only to Christians cannot be gainsaid. But such was the temper of colonial America, the times and the people, that even with that limitation the Toleration Act marked a decided step in advance. The Act came about through a combination of circumstanaces. It reflected the spirit of a Catholic nobleman and a Catholic constituency who were the first to decree freedom of worship and religious tolerance as far as such a condition was possible in the early colonial period. While the Toleration Act was of a limited sort, it contained a germ of that public sentiment which was destined to grow and develop into the spirit which entered into our Federal Constitution of 1787. That spirit still lives in America. It lives in the hearts of Catholics no less than in other right-minded religious groups. It is bound to prevail and by the grace of God, who rules over all of us, it shall prevail.

THOMAS J. WALSH

(How America Lost Half a Continent)

Thomas J. Walsh rose from the humble position of school teacher in a Wisconsin town to United States Senator from Montana, which State he has served in that capacity in Washington since 1913. He was a staunch supporter of President Wilson and constantly advocates America's entry into the League of Nations. Senator Walsh was Chairman of the Democratic National Convention in 1924 and was himself considered as of Presidential potentialities. He is an able debater and one of the most influential members of the upper chamber. When he gets his teeth into corruption, he is as tenacious as a bulldog, and behind his keen blue eyes is unbending integrity. It was he who was chiefly responsible for the uncovering of the Teapot Dome and Elk Hills oil scandals. He is a dry politically, and has the distinction of being a dry personally, as well.

HOW AMERICA LOST HALF A CONTINENT

BY SENATOR THOMAS J. WALSH

I T is the common view of a generation that is passing that its successor possesses less heroic virtues
than characterise the age in which it came upon or
occupied the stage, and quite usual is it to deplore
particularly the decline of religious conviction as a
guiding influence in life.

It may be that the alarm which has been so often
sounded recently over the decline of religious fervour
has no better basis than the old plaint which origi-
nates in the mistaken notion that relaxation in respect to customary observances necessarily implies
a decay of the religious spirit.

However this may be, as in the case of the practise
of any virtue, the day is still distant, if it shall ever
come, when it will be needless to stimulate and cultivate the reverence of man for his Maker and the
observance of the wise law He has ordained to promote the happiness and usefulness of his rational
creatures. Through the ages there has reverberated
the exhortations to those duties by the great Hebrew

teachers. It devolves upon each succeeding generation to see that they do not dwindle into a feeble and
pulseless echo.

George Washington said: "Let us with caution
indulge the supposition that morality can be maintained without religion. Whatever may be conceded
to the influence of refined education on minds of peculiar structure, reason and experience both forbid
us to expect that national morality can prevail in
exclusion of religious principle."

The time has gone by, in this country at least,
when reflecting minds among the devotees of any
creed can regard, except with gratification, movements by those who do not agree with them to en-
large the number of those in whose lives religious
principles constitute a factor and to strengthen the
convictions of those in whom they are an inheritance.
Few will deny that they constitute the great bulwark
of character. There is no denomination but has its
wayward children. Rarely can they be reclaimed at
all except through the efforts of their co-religionists.

The history of our own times, as well as that of
the past, amply demonstrates what a rich source of
genius are Jewish homes. From them have come men
and women eminent in every walk of life, who have
enriched literature and art, delved deeper into science
than had plummet ever sounded, and scattered blessings o'er a smiling land through their discoveries.

Their names are legion and so well known as to make enumeration superfluous.

In the realm of finance they are leaders in every civilised country. How shortsighted is the policy of that nation which would deny itself the contribution to its glory and the comfort and enlightenment of its people of budding geniuses because of their Jewish birth! How pathetic to think of the numberless youths in the ages that have passed who led drab and uneventful lives and passed to unknown graves, who, had they had the help and encouragement, would have done honour to the age in which they lived and conferred inestimable blessings on mankind.

The struggle for religious liberty in this country seems to be unending. The spirit of persecution persists and from time to time flares up with a virulence that seems to transport us back considerably more than a century, directed mainly against the followers of the ancient faith of Israel. The most recent outburst is, it would seem, waning; but, organised more perfectly than some of its predecessors, it may endure sometime. Eventually it must give way before the good sense of the American people.

One hundred and thirty-seven years ago the founders of our government declared in its fundamental law that no religious qualification should ever be required as a requisite for office, having regard as they must have had not only to the plain principles of justice but to the welfare of the nation. The enlightened policy thus announced did not prevail without a struggle.

The liberal statesmen by whom it was advocated did not fail to remind those to whom they appealed, that the army of the Revolution had been recruited from all classes regardless of the faith they professed; that service of the most signal character had been rendered by both Jews and Catholics, who naturally attached themselves to the patriot cause, having found here some measure of liberty at least, and having abundant cause to be at enmity with England.

Popular history has scarcely done justice to either the Jewish or the Catholic heroes of that time that tried men's souls. Every school boy knows about Robert Morris, the financier of the Revolution, but few ever heard of Haym Salomon, the backer of Mr. Morris, who devoted his fortune to the cause of independence and died poor, pointing the moral that republics are ungrateful.

It is quite likely, too, that there was not lost on that generation the lesson of the failure of Canada to join in the insurrection of the other dependencies of Britain. Its people were almost exclusively French and Catholic. Scarcely fifteen years before Lexington they had fought the English invader on the plains of Abraham.

Generations of strife between the country to which they owed allegiance and from which they or other ancestors had come, breaking out from time to time in wars in which they had become involved, had disposed them to revolt, but they held coldly aloof because of the fierce not to say fiendish intolerance of New England. They preferred to tie up with an ancient enemy rather than unite with their neighbours who, though they tolerated the Jew, were unrestrained in persecution of their fellow Christians, the Catholics and Quakers.

Thus *half of the continent of North America was lost* to the United States and a potential enemy left at the doors of the infant Republic.

To the credit of the people of that day it must be said that their gratitude overcame their illiberality, and they made religious freedom the cornerstone of the political system they erected. Not, however, without outcries and imprecations on the part of the intolerant who predicted all manner of evil to the state yet to afflict it, just as the same element in our population, after more than a century and a third has elapsed and toleration is the rule of every advanced nation, insists that the safety of the state requires the exclusion of Catholics and Jews from public office of any grade.

And this immediately following the close of the Great War in which on the bloodiest battlefields the world has ever known, representatives of these sects by the thousands sealed with their blood their devotion to the Stars and Stripes, and organisations of mercy launched by both poured out millions to bring comfort, solace and relief to our men at arms on sea and land without question as to the particular manner in which they worshipped their Maker or their peculiar beliefs in the truths of religion.

There is not a leader of public opinion in the land, save for the obscure promoters of sectarian bigotry, who is not an outspoken champion of the principle of the Constitution on the subject. None of the great journals of the country will give countenance to any other idea. The disseminators of a contrary doctrine hide their identity and operate through secret organisations, shunning the light of day. They assail the objects of their attack not in open debate, where they boldly proclaim their antagonism on religious grounds, but stealthily whisper their slanders into the ears of the ignorant inheritors of the prejudices engendered by the religious wars of remote centuries.

It is a cardinal principle of the philosophy of the age, and none to the contrary is consistent with the spirit of America, that every man is to be judged by his individual worth and not on any basis of either creed or racial derivation.

IRVING LEHMAN

(Constitutional Liberty)

Irving Lehman is a Judge of the Court of Appeals of the State of New York, having been elected to that high office upon the nomination of both the Democratic and Republican parties in 1924, Columbia University, his alma mater, has bestowed upon him the LL.D. degree for achievement at the Bar together with his service as a Justice of the Supreme Court from 1909 to 1913, and now in the highest court of the Commonwealth. It is said of Judge Lehman that "his decisions make law." Throughout his career he has been active in humanitarian endeavour and he is now President of the Jewish Welfare Board. Judge Lehman is a member of The Permanent Commission on Better Understanding.

CONSTITUTIONAL LIBERTY

BY IRVING LEHMAN

WHEN the Congressional representatives of the thirteen colonies issued the Declaration of Independence, they began their explanation of the causes which impelled the people of the colonies to separate from the Mother Country with the words now so familiar to us: "We hold these truths to be self-evident—that all men are created equal; that they are endowed by their Creator with certain inalienable rights; that among these are life, liberty and the pursuit of happiness. That to secure these rights governments are instituted among men, deriving their just powers from the consent of the governed." Not always had such doctrines been regarded as "self-evident truths." Their general acceptance was, indeed, the triumph of the political thought and philosophy of the eighteenth century.

On the sixth day of May, 1776, almost two months before the Declaration of Independence was adopted, a constitutional convention assembled in

Williamsburg, Virginia, to frame a form of government for the new state. Whereupon they adopted a Bill of Rights.

Like the Declaration of Independence, it begins with the assertion "That all men are by nature equally free and independent and have certain inherent rights, of which as they enter into a state of society, they cannot by any compact deprive or divest their posterity; namely, the enjoyment of life and liberty, with the means of acquiring property and pursuing happiness and safety." It then continues with the words: "That all power is vested in, and consequently derived from the People: that the Magistrates are their trustees and servants, and at all times amenable to them. That government is or ought to be instituted for the common benefit, protection and security of the people, nation or community."

The constitution and bill of rights of the Virginia convention is probably the first written instrument creating a government which in terms emanates from the People and which at the same time as it creates the government protects the fundamental rights of the People from encroaching by the State. As might be expected, the enumeration of such fundamental rights embraces those rights which constitute the essence of political liberty according to Anglo-Saxon traditions, rights which by the same traditions were protected by the courts. For the first time, however, religious liberty is included in an enumeration of politcal rights; for the first time in all history has the State recognised and provided by organic law that even the State might not interfere with religious liberty.

Students of our history have frequently noted that, although the colonies were in large part settled by men who sought here the opportunity to worship according to their own conscience, for the most part where the adherents of any sect constituted a considerable majority of the population, they were intolerant of difference of religious opinion. They had made sacrifices to maintain the truth as they saw it. They could not recognise the right of others to maintain the contrary. They regarded as ordained the perdition in the world to come of those who differed with them here; they felt justified in persecuting or at least in placing disabilities upon those who in their opinion were perverse and stubborn in the wrong.

Here and there, it is true, a high measure of religious freedom was achieved. Roger Williams in advance of his time perceived that the State should not interfere in matters of conscience. The settlers of Providence were required to sign a covenant: "We whose names are hereunder written, being desirous of to inhabit in the town of Providence do promise to submit ourselves in active and passive obedience to all such orders or agreements as shall be made for public good of the body in an orderly way by the major consent of the present inhabitants, masters of families incorporated together into a township, and such others as they shall admit into the same *only in civil things.*"

Williams succeeded in obtaining a charter for Rhode Island and Providence Plantations with the provision that "No person within the said colony at any time hereafter shall be in any wise molested, punished or disquieted or called in question for any differences in opinion in matters of religion who do not actually disturb the civil peace of our said colony," and in 1647 the first General Assembly adopted a code of laws which concluded with the words, "All men may walk as their consciences persuade them, every one in the name of God." The charters of Maryland and Pennsylvania too contained provisions safeguarding liberty of conscience, though not in all respects as comprehensive.

Even in these colonies, however, old religious prejudices and religious convictions that were too strong to admit of difference of opinion to some extent thwarted the intentions of the founders, and liberal provisions of laws and charters were at times applied in grudging and narrow spirit. In general it may be said that where the adherents of a particular religion acquired an established church, they placed disabilities upon and even persecuted those who refused to accept the tenets of that church.

Though test acts and statutes imposing civil disabilities because of difference in religious view remained on the books, in practice at the time of the Revolution the Jews at least were under no significant disabilities except in regard to the right to hold public office. Indeed, Jews had been elected to the colonial assemblies in Pennsylvania (David Franks), Georgia (Joseph Ottelenghi), and South Carolina (Francis Salvador), and had been permitted to take their seats without question.

The Virginia Convention met in the atmosphere of enthusiasm for human liberty and against all forms of tyranny which justified the American revolution even in the minds of many who had only with reluctance given up their loyalty to the British crown. All were agreed that in the new state individual liberty must be protected against tyranny by the government. A declaration of rights which "pertain to the People and their posterity as the basis and foundation of government" to be effective must contain more than vague phrases about liberty. To be effective it must contain a definite statement of those rights which the Government must protect and might destroy. The right to set up false gods had never been recognised as inherent in liberty, and men were not then, and are not even to-day, disposed to doubt that those who do not accept their peculiar religious beliefs are in fact setting up false gods. Toleration was sometimes taught as a Christian duty, but in Virginia itself the Church of England was the established church and, not very long before, dissenters had been persecuted. No Anglo-Saxon tradition made religious liberty an "inherent" right of a free people, and the original draft of the Bill of Rights said to have been prepared by George Mason did not contain any provision safeguarding it.

Perhaps the battle which had waged in Virginia in the past over the persecution of dissenters had made men think about the iniquity of attempts to force men's conscience. In the convention were many men who were imbued with a sincere love of liberty in all its phases. It was decided that a provision should be included in the bill of rights to safeguard religious liberty. George Mason accordingly drafted a resolution that "all men should enjoy the fullest toleration in the exercise of religion according to the dictates of conscience." James Madison, a member of that convention, recognised that liberty of thought and conscience must not be confused with toleration but must be demanded as a right.

The substitute resolution offered by Madison protected that right in the fullest manner. "That religion, or the duty we owe our Creator, and the manner of discharging it, being under the direction of reason and conviction only, not of violence or compulsion, all men are equally entitled to the full and free exercise of it, according to the dictates of conscience, and therefore that no man or class of men ought on account of religion to be invested with peculiar emoluments or privileges nor subjected to any penalties or disabilities unless under colour of religion, the preservation of equal liberty, and the existence of the State be manifestly endangered."

The convention agreed that for the word "toleration" the phrase "right of the free exercise of religion" should be substituted, but its members were not willing to go so far as to adopt prohibition of peculiar emoluments or privileges to the adherents of a particular church. In the form finally adopted, this clause reads: "That religion, or the duty we owe to our Creator, and the manner of discharging it can be directed, only by reason and conviction, not by force or violence, and therefore all men are equally entitled to the free exercise of religion according to the dictates of conscience; and that it is the mutual duty of all to practise Christian forbearance, love and charity towards each other."

It would, I think, be impossible to exaggerate the significance of this achievement of the Virginia convention. In formulating the basis of the new State, the bill of rights had confined the powers of the State so that the right of citizens to think and to exercise religion according to the dictates of their conscience must remain inviolate. The convention had recognised that true freedom was not achieved so long as thought and conscience might be fettered. Other constitutions have included provisions which expressed the principle in better form. To Virginia belongs the credit of the adoption of the principle. It is interesting, too, to note that, though the constitutional provision did not prohibit assessments for the support of ministers of a particular church, all movements for such purposes were strenuously and successfully combatted by Jefferson and Madison.

Victory in Virginia acquired particular importance because other colonies or states were about to adopt constitutions for their governance, and could hardly fail to be influenced by the action of the Virginia convention. The issue whether political freedom by its nature includes religious freedom could not be evaded. In each state the question must be met and decided one way or the other.

The Pennsylvania constitution was adopted September 28th, 1776. It contained the provision "That all men have a natural and inalienable right to worship God according to the dictates of their own consciences and understanding, and that no man ought or of right can be compelled to attend any religious worship or erect or support any place of worship or maintain any ministry, contrary to and against his own free will and consent; nor can any man who acknowledges the being of a God be justly deprived of any civil right as a citizen on account of his religious sentiments or peculiar mode of religious worship, and that no authority can or ought to be vested in or assumed by any power that shall in any case interfere with or in any manner control the right of conscience in the free exercise of religious worship."

In some respects this provision goes further and is more definite than the provision in the Virginia convention. It does not, however, admit the right of a citizen to deny conscientiously "the existence of a God," and it is unfortunately to some degree vitiated by inclusion in the constitution of a provision for a test for public office, "That each member of the House of Representatives before taking his seat shall make and subscribe the following declaration: 'I do believe in one God, the creator and governor of the universe, the rewarder of the good and punisher of the wicked, and I do acknowledge the scriptures of the Old and New Testament, to be given by Divine Inspiration. And no further or other religious test shall ever hereafter be required of any civil officer or magistrate in this State.'" Franklin presided at this convention, and as might be supposed he disapproved of the provision of a test for office, but accepted it upon the practical consideration that it might prevent others in the future from imposing a broader test.

The limits of this paper preclude recital of the proceedings of the constitutional convention in each state. The Constitutional Convention held in New York in 1777, however, should not be entirely omitted. The original draft of the provision for religious freedom, prepared by a committee of which John Jay, William Duer, Gouverneur Morris, Robert R. Livingston and Abraham Yates were members, contained the phrase that "free toleration be forever allowed." Before adoption by the convention it was changed, as in Virginia, to "free exercise and enjoyment of religious profession and worship." Originally this was offered "to all denominations of Christians, without preference or distinction, and to all Jews, Turks and Infidels," subject to limitation where the Legislature might determine particular doctrine "incompatible with and repugnant to the peace, safety and welfare of civil society in general and of this State in particular."

This provision was amended in the committee itself in a most liberal spirit, but the debates in the convention evinced a spirit of doubt as to the doctrines of the Roman Catholic Church on the part of some sections of the State and some members, which is even now not entirely dead. John Jay himself proposed an amendment that to the general provision for religious freedom an exception should be inserted that "professors of the religion of the Church of Rome" should not be permitted to "hold lands in or be admitted to a participation of the civil rights enjoyed by the members of this State, until such time as the said professors shall appear in the Supreme Court of this State and there most solemnly swear that they verily believe in their consciences that no Pope, priest or foreign authority on earth hath power to absolve the subjects of this State from their allegiance to the same. And further that they renounce and believe to be false and wicked the dangerous and damnable doctrine that the Pope or any other earthly authority have power to absolve men from sins described in and prohibited by the Holy Gospel of Jesus Christ, and particularly that no Pope, priest or foreign authority on earth has power to absolve them from the obligation of their oath."

Perhaps it would be wrong to give too much significance to Jay's attitude. His Huguenot ancestry naturally tended to prejudice him against the Catholics. His English traditions led him to justify the then prevailing English practice of Catholic persecution.

It seems to me of far more significance that the Convention under the leadership of Gouverneur

Morris and Chancellor Livingstone defeated the amendment by a vote of nineteen to ten and finally adopted a resolution in ringing words: "And whereas we are required by the benevolent principles of rational liberty, not only to expel civil tyranny, but also to guard against that spiritual oppression and intolerance wherewith the bigotry and ambition of weak and wicked priests and princes have scourged mankind, this convention doth further in the name and by the authority of the good people of this State, ordain, determine and declare that the free exercise and enjoyment of religious profession and worship without discrimination or preference, shall forever hereafter be allowed within this State to all mankind. Provided that the liberty of conscience hereby granted shall not be so construed as to excuse acts of licentiousness."

Well may we say that, because America led the way, religious freedom seems natural to us now.

The labour of the men who in the constitutional convention of the separate states had succeeded in obtaining recognition of the principle that religious liberty was an inherent right of free citizens with which the State might not interfere received its crown when the Constitution of the United States was adopted with its prohibition against all religious tests and its brief but all-inclusive provision in the First Amendment that "Congress shall make no laws

respecting an establishment of religion or prohibiting
the free exercise thereof."

I have no intention of attempting to go beyond
the subject of this paper in order to trace even briefly
the ebb and flow of tides of public opinion in the
United States in regard to religious prejudices. The
great leaders of thought and action during the Revolution, Washington and Franklin, Jefferson and
Madison, were all men of splendid liberality of
thought and spirit, who could perceive that thought
and conscience cannot be constrained, and that a
civil government may not enter into realms where
constraint is both undesirable and impossible. They
succeeded in making men of lesser minds see that
freedom of thought and conscience is a matter of
right and not of favour. They embodied that principle in the fundamental law of the country, and that
is perhaps the greatest contribution which America
has made to political thought and ideals and practice. They gave practical effect to Paine's words,
though some of them abhorred Paine's religious
views: *"Toleration is not the opposite of intolera-
tion, but the counterfeit of it.* Both are despotisms.
The one assumes the right of withholding liberty of
conscience, and the other of granting it. Who then
art thou, vain dust and ashes, by whatever name thou
art called, whether a king or bishop, a church or a
state, a parliament or anything else, that obtrudes

thine insignificance between the soul of a man and his maker? Mind thine own concern."

It is a trite saying that government is not merely a matter of law but of men. As the very foundation of our government, the organic law decrees freedom of thought and conscience, yet from time to time men try to destroy or abridge the freedom which the law decrees. It has been said that no man is worthy of freedom who cannot defend it. We celebrated, in 1927, the one hundred and fiftieth anniversary of the recognition of religious freedom as a legal right. We rejoice and are proud because we are citizens of the country which has recognised that right and guaranteed it in its constitution. We prove ourselves worthy of it when we are ready to defend it from direct or indirect attack, when we fight all forms of prejudice, whether directed against us or others, which threaten it.

MITCHELL SALEM FISHER

(An Excursion for Sages)

Mitchell Salem Fisher is one of the younger men in the rabbinate. He is ministering to the historic and venerable Rodeph Sholom Congregation in New York City. Graduated from New York University with highest academic honors, he pursued post-graduate work at Columbia and the University of Chicago. At New York University he won the Ogden Butler Classical Fellowship for proficiency in Greek and Latin. He also represented New York University on the team which debated the Universities of Oxford, Sheffield, and Edinburgh abroad. He is national vice-president of the Student Zionist Organisation of America. His special field of study is philosophy and he has written monographs on John Stuart Mill and Robert Boyle.

AN EXCURSION FOR SAGES

BY MITCHELL SALEM FISHER

BETTER understanding necessitates a breaking away from prejudice and preconceived opinion, a free and unfettered excursion of the mind. The history of philosophy shows how this excursion of the mind aided peoples to comprehend each other, emphasised the essential unity of man as a thinking and rational being, and thereby contributed toward a tolerance of different opinions and varying creeds. Before the advent of philosophy we had blind faith. With the coming of the philosophic spirit man's eyes were opened, and though at times, as in the Middle Ages, dark prejudice was to obstruct his vision, intellectual honesty was added as a factor in the obliteration of racial and religious barriers. Israel gave the prophet; Greece the philosopher. Both have developed better understanding, the former by emphasising the ideal of justice, the latter by holding high the torch of truth.

A certain rhetorician of the ancient Sophists named

Alcidamas said, "God made all men free; Nature made none a slave." These early liberals would recognise no far-reaching, elemental difference between races and social groups. Their broad liberal spirit influenced literature through Euripides and the poets of the new comedy. Even Herodotus, with all his pious credulity, was liberalised by their teachings. Enlightened by the sophistic spirit, Herodotus travels through the ancient world, and succeeds in shaking off his old local prejudices. When he learns how the "mad" Cambyses killed the calf-god, he expresses a good-natured skepticism concerning the reasons why a Persian king should thus despise Egyptian animal worship. "Custom," said Herodotus in the genial manner of the Greek, "custom is lord of all." How we might wish that men in all ages had taken that tolerant point of view, and had not made custom into caste!

Socrates made the next great contribution to the cause of better understanding. He may rightly be called the intellectual father of our civilisation. Clear and reasoned thinking, he held, would end all prejudices. When men will think, when men will truly know, they cannot help being virtuous, just and kind. "I do nothing," says Socrates in the Apology, "but go about persuading you all, old and young alike, not to take thought for your persons or properties, but first and chiefly to care about the greatest improvement of the soul."

If men in all ages had listened to him, had forgotten their petty persons and properties, had cared deeply for the soul's improvement, the disease of prejudice would have been long ago stamped out.

The Cynics and Stoics, rather than Plato and Aristotle, the two illustrious followers of Socrates, continue the tradition of better understanding. Diogenes, the Cynic, was a man of the world, who undertook much labour and bodily suffering to bring a closer sympathy between men and groups. For example, when taken prisoner, he did not regret Athens, but tried to improve even the pirates, among whom he was cast. On being sold, he lived as complacently in Corinth as he had before in Athens. In those days as in ours, when great crowds would gather at a national or international mart, men would ask the strangers, "Of what city are you?" The answer would be "of Athens" by one, "of Sparta," another, "of Thebes," a third. But when Socrates and Diogenes as well as many others were asked that current question they answered, "Of the universe." Patriotism did not blind their eyes to the essential unity of man. They were courageous leaders in the field of better understanding. Not that these men were disloyal to their native city or state. Socrates willingly submitted to Athenian law and drank the hemlock; Zeno and Cleanthes declined the citizenship of Athens lest they should be taught to hold cheap their birthplaces; and among the Romans Seneca frequently emphasises the concept that every man is born into two communities, his native city and the cosmopolis.

But above class, city, and creed the Stoics advanced a splendid cosmopolitan ideal. It was and is one of the greatest gifts philosophy has presented to the cause of better understanding. It permitted local loyalties, but it held up at the same time an ideal of a world-state from which only brute animals would be excluded, an ideal society in which all distinctions of race, caste, class, and sect are to be subordinated to kinship, brotherhood, and fraternity.

The best known of the Stoics were Seneca (3-65 A. C. E.), Epictetus (first century), and the Emperor Marcus Aurelius (121-180). All three may be considered as having been workers in the cause of better understanding. Seneca writes in one of his letters to Lucilius: " 'They are slaves,' people declare. Nay, rather they are men. 'Slaves!' No, comrade. 'Slaves!' No, they are unpretentious friends. . . . Kindly remember that he whom you call your slave sprang from the same stock, is smiled upon by the same skies, and on equal terms with yourself breathes, lives, and dies."

The true Stoic hated slavery. The true Stoic lived

and worked for a commonwealth in which all men should be free. "He who has observed with intelligence the administration of the world," exclaimed Epictetus, "and has learned that the greatest and supreme and the most comprehensive community is that which is composed of men and God, and that from God have descended the seeds, not only to my father and grandfather, but to *all* beings who are generated on the earth, and particularly to rational beings—why should not such a man call himself a citizen of the world, why not a son of God?" As children of the same God, Epictetus wanted men of all creeds and classes to recognise their brotherhood. One of his listeners could not appreciate this universalism, still wanted sectarian divisions to be upheld, and asked the philosopher how might a man eat acceptably to the gods. Epictetus answered, and his words may well come ringing their message even to the men of our day, "If he can eat justly and contentedly, and with equanimity, and temperately and orderly, will it not be also acceptable to the gods? . . . will you not bear with your own brother, who has Zeus for his progenitor, and is like a son from the same seeds and of the same descent from above?" The soul of mankind might not have been stained by the blood of the Inquisition had the words of Epictetus been understood, appreciated, and followed!

No less a man than Marcus Aurelius, the emperor-philosopher, was the next pioneer in the cause of better understanding. He introduced humane Stoic principles into Roman law. The Talmud speaks of intercourse between one of the Antonines and Judah ha-Nasi, in which the Roman emperor showed marked respect for the Jewish prince. This emperor who showed such respect for a man of different creed, was probably Aurelius. It is to be doubted if the appeal to sweep away our prejudices and recognise our common brotherhood, has ever been couched in more cogent phrase than that of this emperor. We can marvel at his words, "Cast away from thee opinion and thou art safe. . . . Hast thou forgotten how closely all men are allied one to another by a kindred, not of blood, nor of seed, but of the same mind? Thou hast also forgotten that every man's mind partakes of the Deity and issueth from thence, and that no man can properly call anything his own, no, not his son, nor his body, nor his life, for they all proceed from that One who is the giver of all things: that all things are but opinions."

One would wish that philosophy had continued the Stoic tradition. Unfortunately for the cause of tolerance, philosophy now became the handmaiden of the Christian faith. Man's mind was no longer free. One believed, or one was a heretic with whom it was dangerous even to converse. The most liberal philos-

ophers of these truly dark ages never extended their
understanding beyond the circle of the European
nations, and never included the Jews. The church
simply refused to understand other creeds. Only one
religion was right; all others were works of the devil,
to be uprooted and suppressed. St. Augustine's "City
of God" called its citizens from all races and its pil-
grims "from men of every tongue," but his City of
God admitted only Catholics. Until modern times
philosophic writing does little for real tolerance.
Bruno, Savonarola and men like them were martyred
for their faith, but even they did not possess much of
the truly cosmopolitan spirit.

Thomas More is probably the first to continue
the work of Sophist and Stoic, although Grotius with
his emphasis on "Natural right" undoubtedly was
conscious of some higher ideal than that of narrow
nationalism. In the "Utopia," published in 1516,
More describes his idea of a perfect state. Utopians
are to be largely pantheists, but they are never to
resort to violence, or to have any obstinate conten-
tions as to which religion is best. More visions the result of this beautiful religious freedom, and foresees
a public religious service in which each sectarian
would participate in his own way. Yet the service
would be so expressive of common brotherhood that
all would consider it an impiety to enter, without
first purging their minds and spirits of all racial and

religious prejudices. He saw a glorious people garbed
in white, entering a magnificent temple where in an
atmosphere fragrant with frankincense and other
sweet spices they would pray together in the brotherhood of man. Those customs or religious rites peculiar to each man's religion would be observed pri-
vately at home. In the public service of the Utopians, prayers "are so composed, that whatsoever is
pronounced by the whole assembly may be likewise
applied to every man in particular to his own condition." Thus did the social dreamer More try to
make religion not a source of divisiveness and hatred
as it has so often been in human history, but a tie
binding the hands and hearts of men in a social unity
and brotherhood, a true vital agency for the spiritual
advance of man.

Tomaso Campanella, another great soul who la-
boured in the cause of man's brotherhood, recognises
in his "City of the Sun" no class distinctions save that
of knowledge. On the other hand, some of the Utopians, as James Harrington in his "Oceana," were less
liberal, and took the trouble to exclude Jews from
their ideal commonwealth. The battle for better understanding was not yet won.

Modern philosophy taken as a whole, representing as it does the revolt of the inquiring spirit against
the shackles of the scholastic spirit is winning the
battle. It has been a tremendous force in the evolu-

tion of a fearlessly liberal attitude, perhaps the most important force in the history of man.

Francis Bacon (1561-1626), was really the first to vision the needs of modern times. He declared that mankind must have a *novum organum*, a new logic. To do that men must first clear their minds of that dark prejudiced ignorance which is the source of all human suffering. Men must strike down the four "idols," their false preconceived notions. Among those idols Bacon mentions as one of the most important the "idola specus" or idols of the den, whereby men think that their own faiths and beliefs brook no toleration of others. With John Locke, a follower of Bacon, who through Voltaire and Montesquieu profoundly influenced our American revolution and the American ideal of religious liberty, the problem of understanding becomes paramount. Indeed, his chief work is called "An Essay Concerning Human Understanding." Locke proclaimed there was no inborn truth and that all men were by nature "free, equal, and independent." Understand and you shall know that you are brethren! Better understanding brings a better world.

Both schools of pre-Kantian philosophy, the rationalists in which Descartes, Spinoza, Malebranche, Leibnitz, and Wolff were members, and the empiricist led by Bacon, Hobbes, Locke, Berkeley and Hume, contributed mightily in the cause of rapprochement between nations and creeds. Yet it must be stated that our cause has drawn strength rather from the latter than from the former. Rationalism tended to enshrine preconceived notions; empiricism was ruthless in its tolerance. Although Spinoza belongs in the former school, his life and thought have contributed tremendously toward the cause of the liberal. Especially did the excommunication of Spinoza bring to the Jew of later days the realisation that a broader spirit of tolerance was necessary toward philosophers, and toward representatives of other faiths, while to the world at large Spinoza's "Tractatus theologico-politicus" yet remains one of the clearest, fairest, and most thoughtful pleas for freedom of thought and faith. The true philosopher has ever stood with the true prophet, pointing the way toward that ideal state in which all men shall really clasp the hand of brotherhood. Truth as well as justice must finally make all men comrades. Philosophy in our day is a treasured handmaiden of better understanding.

ISAAC LANDMAN

(Better Understanding in the Bible)

Vigorous spokesman of enlightened Judaism and vigilant defender of American liberties, Rabbi Landman is an able pleader for both these cherished ideals, whether his message be from the pulpit, forum, or editorial sanctum. Courage is a trait intrinsic in his character, and while no denunciation can swerve him from a cause he deems right, his work has been essentially for concord and unity, not only among the factions of modern Israel, but likewise for better understanding between followers of the three major creeds in America. As editor of The American Hebrew he organised the Permanent Commission on Better Understanding which functions with much influence to allay religious rancours and to scotch unfounded slanders when such arise, unjustly stigmatising any religious group in America. As playwright, author, and editor, Rabbi Landman has won deserved prestige. His activities have been as varied as his personality is versatile.

W. H. B.

BETTER UNDERSTANDING IN THE BIBLE

BY ISAAC LANDMAN

IT would be a shocking admission to those who
accept the Bible as the literal word of God, therefore holding between its covers all of revealed truth,
that within its pages there is no formulated ideal of
mutual understanding among peoples and nations
and creeds. But this admission is true. Liberals in
religion will not be surprised. They hold that the
Bible is a continuous revelation which is by no means
concluded. All the truth and the spiritual outreach-
ings of mankind are not exclusively within its con-
fines. New revelations are constantly being vouchsafed us for the salvation of mankind.

The aspiration for comity and mutuality among
peoples and nations and creeds is one of these new
revelations. It sprang from the woes and sorrows of
the recent world conflict. It is uniquely a modern
ideal and is the fruit of human reactions to the racial
and national narrowness and bitterness which culminated in the Great War. Therefore, no Bible
writer could have anticipated such a hope.

Students of the Bible as an historical document, not as a revealed, literally true book, will hold with the Liberals. And such a position does not detract from the Bible's values for modern man. That Bible authors could not grasp the thought of better understanding among peoples and nations and creeds is self-evident: the concepts of what peoples are in the modern sense, and nations and creeds, were foreign to the ancient, oriental mind.

Each people deemed itself the chosen darling of its God. Each nation had its own pet deity. There were no creeds as we understand the word today. Jahveh, the God of the Hebrews, for example, was concerned only with the Hebrews and they with him; and Asshur retained the same relationship with the Assyrians; and Marduk with the Babylonians. The enemy of the nation was the enemy of the deity. They who blasphemed the deity had to account to his nation. It was the philosophy of religious nationalism which made the deity map-limited, soil-bound. Unity, mutuality, concord among peoples and races and religions not united under the aegis of the same divinity was unthinkable.

And yet, so unique is that sacred library of the Jews and the Christians, so wide the experiences of man's adjustment to the universe recorded therein, so deep the insight of its spiritual geniuses that this modern story of Better Understanding, the first chapter of which is only now being written in the Occidental world, finds its roots sunk deep there, crudely and groping, of course, but doubtless there.

Anyone who is at all well read in the Bible, who is fortunate to have stored up in his own mind at least some of the most salient passages, will readily call up such brilliant, universalistic flashes as Malachi's question:

> "Have we not all one father?
> Hath not one God created us?"

Or St. Paul's all-inclusive, all-illuminating statement to the Athenians: "The God that made the world and all nations therein . . . hath made of one blood all nations and men to dwell upon the face of the earth."

Malachi, however, is the last of the great Prophets in the Bible, and St. Paul delivered his address to the Greeks in the second half of the first Christian century. They were building upon the human experiences that had gone before. The influence of the Hebrew Prophets was already leavening the life of the Western world. Their autobiographies were collected, and those who could might read. Malachi's query was the crystallisation of about six centuries of prophetic gropings into the mysteries of human relationships with God. St. Paul's novel pronouncement grew out of the contemplations of a keen Jewish mind, making fearless incursions into Greek culture and religion.

It is to be assumed, therefore, that the predecessors of these two spiritual heroes must have had somewhat to say which, in the minds of Malachi and Paul of Tarsus, took the shape of these flashes of universal good-will and understanding. The Bible testifies that this is so. Among the law-givers and prophets of Jewish Scriptures there are to be discerned occasional hints of fundamentals regarding this ideal upon which man may build even to-day. And, although the Letters of Paul and the Gospels are mainly propaganda literature in behalf of the struggling new faith, sufficient of the sayings of Jesus have been preserved in these books to light the dark way to the broad road of better understanding among men.

What is presented here is not an exhaustive study of Jewish and Christian Scriptures on this engrossing theme; nor is an attempt being made to interpret Scriptures so as to extract from the Holy Writ all the possibilities homiletic license permits. Here at random are assembled indications for a possible study, if nothing more. What follows is literally a collection of flash-backs into the minds of the Bible's spiritual geniuses. Here are given the roots of a compelling universal hope, which is beginning to clothe itself in the flesh and spirit of organised endeavour toward mutuality and understanding among peoples and nations and creeds as these have developed in the modern era.

Tradition accords the authorship of the Pentateuch to Moses. Modern Bible critics deny the historical authenticity of this tradition. Sentimentally, one should abhor these critics. They are destroying the delightful legend of Moses, fourteen centuries or so before the Common Era, painting the background for the present story of better understanding. But truth batters through sentiment; vaults tradition.

Place, then, the Book of Leviticus, for instance, at whatever date the critics may please, and accord the authorship to whomsoever the critics may choose. The truth, nevertheless, crashes through to the fact that in the midst of presently obsolete Levitical laws, we find ideals that are fundamental to better understanding, such as these:

"Thou shalt love thy neighbour as thyself."
"Thou shalt not hate thy brother in thy heart."
"Thou shalt not respect the person of the poor, nor favour the person of the mighty; but in righteousness shalt thou judge thy neighbour."

Probably there are no greater and insurmountable stumbling blocks to better understanding among peoples and nations than the fear and suspicion of aliens. One may perhaps assign a measure of accountability for such fear and suspicion to the very Pentateuch with its concepts of national deities and chosen peoples. Psychology, however, would trace fear and suspicion centuries back of anything written in the Bible. Whatever one's judgment may be on these origins, it is patent that the regard and care for the alien as taught in Leviticus, if these were universally practised to-day, would contribute tremendously to the dissipation of these fears and add to the constructive upbuilding of better understanding. Our modern term "alien" is "stranger" in the Bible. The two quotations that follow are examples of many, enacted into law by the Hebrews as a result of their sad experiences in lands where they themselves were "strangers" or aliens":

"Love ye therefore the stranger; for ye were strangers in the land of Egypt."

"The stranger that sojourneth with you shall be unto you as the home-born among you, and thou shalt love him as thyself."

The real essence of Bible idealism, however, is contained in the Prophets, not in the Pentateuch. There are those who interpret the Prophets as fore-tellers of incidents and things that pertain to Christianity. There are those who insist with equal inter-pretive sincerity that the Prophets were forth-tellers of ideals without any special reference to Christ or Christianity. Here, however, we are on safe and non-controversial ground. Notwithstanding that we quote mainly from the Prophet Isaiah,

theologically the most controversial of them all, we
cull selections, inspired pronouncements as they
seem to us, in which there is inherent the hope of
good-will and better understanding.

> "They shall beat their swords into plowshares,
> And their spears into pruning-hooks;
> Nation shall not lift up sword against nation,
> Neither shall they learn war any more."

To which Micah added:

> "But they shall sit every man under his vine and
>   under his fig-tree;
> And none shall make them afraid."

And again Isaiah:

> "And the wolf shall dwell with the lamb,
> And the leopard shall lie down with the kid;
> And the calf and the young lion and the fatling
>   together;
> And a little child shall lead them."

There is one passage at least in this superb
Prophet's writing which even critics might declare
to be a definite statement on the present day hope
for concord and mutuality among races and peoples,
namely:

> "In that day shall Israel be the third with Egypt and with
> Assyria, a blessing in the midst of the earth; for that the Lord
> of hosts hath blessed him, saying: 'Blessed be Egypt My
> people, and Assyria the work of My hands, and Israel Mine
> inheritance.'"

From the Gospels we select, first of all, the stirring proclamation, "Peace on earth and good-will to men." And from those utterances credited to Jesus:

"Love your enemies and pray for them that persecute you."
"Why beholdest thou the mote that is in thy brother's eye, but considerest not the beam that is in thine own eye?"
"Whatsoever ye would that men should do unto you, even so do ye also unto them; for this is the law and the Prophets."

One thing is certain when we view the present scene. The Prophet Hosea was correct when he said, "The people that is without understanding is distraught." Certainly there is hope for better understanding if we would give ear to Isaiah's, "Come let us reason together." In this phrase Isaiah may be suggesting the *will* to better understanding. And from the New Testament the well-known declaration, "By their fruits ye shall know them."

At any rate, to those who are eager that better understanding may eventuate among all nations and men that dwell upon the face of the earth, the Bible offers the cheering advice Moses gave to Joshua when the latter entered upon the task of conquering the promised land: "Be strong and of good courage."

THE PERMANENT COMMISSION ON
BETTER UNDERSTANDING BETWEEN
CHRISTIANS AND JEWS IN AMERICA

S. Parkes Cadman

Henry Morgenthau

Victor J. Dowling

Francis P. Duffy

W. H. P. Faunce

Irving Lehman

Stephen S. Wise

Roscoe Pound

Martin Conboy

THE PERMANENT COMMISSION ON
BETTER UNDERSTANDING

THE Permanent Commission on Better Understanding between Christians and Jews in America is composed of Protestants, Catholics and Jews. Its function is limited to this: whenever a group of American citizens comes before the Commission claiming that it is attacked unjustly and on grounds that are ill-founded; that the attack is calculated to engender ill-will and breed hate, with no redress under law or at the hands of the Government, the Permanent Commission on Better Understanding investigates, ascertains and enunciates the truth—creates and voices public opinion on the subject.

The members of this Commission are not official representatives of their organised religious denominations, but volunteers—men of enlightenment, of tested moral calibre, of sympathetic understanding of the convictions of others—lovers of truth and of their fellowmen. It is free of private religious views or doctrines or beliefs or practises. There is thus entailed no loss whatever of the integrity of the three separate religious bodies. It is free of politics. It does not initiate any new movements. It does not, of its own accord, investigate any problem that may trouble the religious groups. Questions touching international relations are entirely out of its province. The purpose and objective of this Commission, therefore, is solely opinion-making. It has no permanent officers and calls itself into session only when it receives an appeal to redress a group wrong. It determines for itself whether a protest from a particular group comes within its purview. But when it undertakes a task, when it investigates painstakingly, and when it speaks after careful and unbiased deliberation, the whole nation listens and accepts its pronouncement as the enlightened voice of the Protestant, Catholic and Jewish population, on the broad grounds of American humanity.

The Commission, organised April 15, 1927, is the crystallisation of the editorial policy of *The American Hebrew*, launched by this magazine to combat the antagonisms engendered by post-war misunderstandings in America. It is composed of nine men, representing the three major faiths: Dr. S. Parkes Cadman, Martin Conboy, Esq., Hon. Victor J. Dowling, Father Francis P. Duffy, Dr. W. H. P. Faunce, Hon. Irving Lehman, Hon. Henry Morgenthau, Dean Roscoe Pound, Dr. Stephen S. Wise; Isaac Landman is secretary.

FIRST PUBLIC PRONOUNCEMENT OF
THE PERMANENT COMMISSION

IN THE TOWN of Massena, New York, on
Saturday, September 22nd, 1928, two days before the Jewish Day of Atonement, Barbara Griffith, the four-year-old daughter of David Griffith,
disappeared. An exhaustive search by the parents,
police, firemen and private citizens of the town
failed to reveal her whereabouts. Due to the ignorance and gullibility of the Mayor and a state
trooper, a rumour spread that the Jews probably
kidnapped the child for ritual purposes.

A serious situation for the Jews of Massena was
momentarily created when at noon, the next day, the
child still unfound, Rabbi Berel Brennglass and
officials of the synagogue were confronted by a state
trooper with the question whether Jews offer human
sacrifice on a holiday, implying the old ritual murder charge. Rabbi Brennglass pronounced the question ridiculous and asked the officials whether they
realised the seriousness of the query put to him.
The situation, however, was relieved at 4:30 that
afternoon when the child was found in a forest about

a mile from her home. The child informed the police that she had gone into the woods on Saturday, had become lost, had slept through the night and feared to go home by herself.

The Jews of Massena, through their courageous Rabbi, communicated with Mr. Louis Marshall of New York, as President of the American Jewish Committee, and with Rabbi Stephen S. Wise, as President of the American Jewish Congress, both of whom in public letters vigorously denounced the stupidity of the Massena officials. Governor Smith likewise called the state police officer to task. Thereupon both the mayor and the state trooper apologised to Rabbi Brennglass, to the Massena Jewish community and to the Jews of America.

In order to forestall the recurrence of the blood ritual libel in America, the Permanent Commission on Better Understanding between Christians and Jews in America deemed it timely to issue a pronouncement, and, on October 5th, 1928, the press of the country carried the following:

FELLOW AMERICANS:

WERE it not for the far-reaching menace implied in the blood ritual accusation against the Jews, raised for the first time on American soil, this barbarous charge would not merit the dignity of a public statement by the Permanent Commission on Better Understanding Between Christians and Jews in America. However, the history of persecution resulting from religious canards proves that, once started, these false rumours swiftly spread and are virtually impossible of extirpation. Only last month this hideous blood accusation raised its head in Germany, Poland and Jugo-Slavia.

The incident which occurred in the village of Massena, New York, on the eve of the Day of Atonement, September 23rd, when the heads of the Jewish congregation were interrogated concerning what proved to be the temporary disappearance of a four-year-old Christian girl, as if there might be some relation between her disappearance and the alleged blood-ritual practise, moves this Commission, representing Protestants, Catholics and Jews, to declare this age old accusation to be false. It is, moreover, cruel and unconscionable—an abhorrent fiction, calculated to transplant into American minds a long-refuted mediaeval libel that has been the cause of untold suffering and repeated acts of bloodshed in the Old World.

Since the twelfth century, Jews in various countries of Europe have been accused of using Christian blood for ritual purposes; and, to obtain this blood, to commit assault upon and even to murder Christian children for that purpose. More than one hundred and thirty such accusations are recorded since the year 1144; in each case the accusation was incontrovertibly proved to have been falsely conceived and maliciously spread. So horrible and monstrous is this charge that the best minds of all ages and creeds, including Popes, founders of the Reformation and statesmen, have denounced it and publicly warned against its further dissemination.

As late as 1840, fifty-eight Jewish converts to Christianity, headed by the Bishop of the Anglican Church at Jerusalem, solemnly protested that "we have never directly or indirectly heard, much less known, among the Jews of the practise of killing Christians or using Christian blood, and we believe this charge, so often brought against them formerly and now lately revived, to be a foul and Satanic falsehood. Emperors, too, were outraged at this accusation, and Frederick the Great of Germany exonerated the Jews, "from the grave crime with which they have been charged," declaring "the Jews of Germany clear from all suspicion."

The Permanent Commission on Better Understanding Be-

*tween Christians and Jews in America, supported by most
thorough and authoritative investigation on the part of Protestant, Catholic and Jewish scholars, solemnly affirm that
the blood accusation is a cruel and utterly baseless libel on
Judaism; that there is no custom, ceremony or ritual among
Jews anywhere, no more than there is among Christians anywhere, and nothing in their traditions or literature, which
calls for the use of human blood for any purpose; that in
the whole of the varied and vicissitudinous history of the
Jews throughout the world there has never been, nor is
there to-day, even a sect of Judaism that has observed so
barbarous and inhuman a practise.*

*High-minded Americans had believed that the seeds of so
false and monstrous an accusation against the Jews could
no more find soil in America than could the stupidities of
witchcraft be revived.*

*The Massena incident, therefore, moves the Permanent
Commission on Better Understanding to urge our fellow
citizens throughout the nation, in the interest of true religion and of our common devotion to our native country, to
prevent the spread of this libel on the Jews, to destroy it by
the ridicule it deserves, and forestall its recurrence by enlightenment, lest ill-will and religious enmity spread among
our citizenry and discord disrupt our national life.*

*(Signed) William H. P. Faunce, Chairman; S. Parkes
Cadman, Martin Conboy, Victor J. Dowling, Francis
P. Duffy, Irving Lehman, Henry Morgenthau, Roscoe
Pound, Stephen S. Wise; Isaac Landman, Secretary.*

The Commission, the membership of which is now
being augmented, hopes that the occasions will be
few when there shall be need of an utterance on its
part. Indeed, the Commission would consider its purpose achieved if no necessity arose for a statement.
However, the Commission stands prepared to lay low
any ill-founded attacks upon the Protestant, Catholic
or Jewish groups in America.